WOMEN IN AMERICAN SOCCER AND EUROPEAN FOOTBALL: DIFFERENT ROADS TO SHARED GLORY

BY

ANDREI S. MARKOVITS

This book constitutes a work all its own. It is a completely revised, massively updated and substantially expanded text based on my previously published piece "A Silent 'Feminization' of Global Sports Cultures? Women as Soccer Players in Europe and America" that appeared as Chapter 4 in my book *GAMING THE WORLD: How Sports are Reshaping Global Politics and Culture* co-authored with Lars Rensmann and published by Princeton University Press in 2010. I asked for and received full permission from Princeton University Press to use segments of Chapter 4 to publish the current work provided I featured the following text by the Press at this work's outset. I hereby do so!

Table of Contents

PREFACE and ACKNOWLEDGMENTS

I have always been struck by gate crashers. Much of my academic research and writing over the past 50 years has focused on such: be they labor unions and new social movements in Germany and Austria; or Jews confronting anti-Semitism in these two countries and beyond. My last two books dealt with women's agency and their growing voices in two crucial areas of social change. Unsurprisingly, I co-authored them with two young women, both of whom were among my most brilliant undergraduate students at the University of Michigan: The first book entitled *Sportista: Female Fandom in the United States*, published by Temple University Press in 2012 and co-authored with Emily Albertson, centered on how women have come to crash the male bastion of sports both as producers – i.e. athletes; but also as consumers – i.e. fans. The second book was called *From Property to Family: American Dog Rescue and the Discourse of Compassion.* Published by the University of Michigan Press in 2014 and co-authored with Katherine Crosby, this book focused on the absolutely central role that women have historically played in the protection of animals as well as the disempowered and marginalized and forgotten in the human world. Being the consistent advocates of the weak and disenfranchised, women have always been democratizing agents by dint of advocating for the inclusion of the hitherto excluded. After all, the constant process of democratization always entails the inclusion of the formerly excluded as agents with their own voices as well as their own fully accepted sovereignty and integrity.

There can be no doubt that the events that emerged in the late 1960s represented a major inclusive step in all advanced industrial democracies. Poignantly focused on the year "1968" – indeed the Germans have come to call this politically significant generation the "achtundsechziger" with the French following suit with their synonymous "soixante-huitards" – nothing proved as crucial in its social significance among these "sixty-eighters" than the second wave of feminism. Arguably more consequential in all aspects of society than its predecessor of the late 19th and early 20th centuries (the so-called first wave of feminism), the second wave brought women into the public sphere like no force before. Sport, a particularly tenacious male preserve, was surely among the most prominent spheres which women entered by dint of the changes wrought by this wave of feminism. More specifically still, and socially much more significantly, women not only entered sports but indeed the cultural bastions of male consumption and masculine identity such as ball-centered team sports, perhaps Association football (soccer) being among the most prominent among them.

Ever since my childhood in Romania, I have always been deeply interested in soccer and other ball-centered team sports. Among many major events such as Champions League finals and EURO tournaments,

I have been fortunate to attend five World Cups on the men's side – 1966, 1974, 1982, 1994, 2006 – and three on the women's – 1999, 2003, 2011. In the latter, I followed the United States women's national team to all the cities in which it played in the tournament in Germany. It all began in Dresden with a win against North Korea followed by another win against Colombia in Hoffenheim. Then, a rather surprising loss to archrival Sweden happened in Wolfsburg leading to the United States ending the round robin phase of the tournament in second place to Sweden's first which meant that Team USA now had to face formidable Brazil already in the quarterfinals instead of later in the tournament. This again happened in Dresden. Abby Wambach's legendary header in that game on the end of a dream cross by Megan Rapinoe tying the match against Marta and Company in the 123rd minute will forever remain one of my most prized memories from the myriad of sporting events that I have attended or watched on two continents over 65 years. Winning the ensuing penalty contest against Brazil catapulted the Americans to face the French in a semifinal match in Mönchengladbach that the United States won handily. Onward to the final in Frankfurt where the heavily favored American team outplayed Japan for the duration of the match but still lost the title in a heartbreaker. That is sport! In a way it was so much nicer attending these women's world cups than the men's. The atmosphere at these women's tournaments was always positive and celebratory and inclusive, with the fans smiling and happy exactly the very opposite of the men's competitions that have always featured anger, derision, aggression and hostilities based on much-invoked nationalist symbols featuring alleged historical resentments and slights that the team's victory on the field would inevitably ameliorate if not erase. Such ugly scenes were very much in evidence even at the allegedly harmonious and welcoming World Cup in Germany in the summer of 2006, the competition that allowed the Germans to finally shed their falsely purported Holocaust-imposed reticence to express their national pride and wave the flag just like everybody else did. They, of course, always could and did way before this competition. I have, over the years, written books and papers on women's and men's world cups and have always come to see the women's game as an integral part of this great sport.

As a student of comparative politics and political sociology, my work has also centered on a constant comparison of things European and American. Thus, it is no accident that my work on soccer has also focused on this aspect of the game. In a chapter in my book co-authored with Lars Rensmann entitled *Gaming the World: How Sports Are Reshaping Global Politics and Culture* published by Princeton University Press in 2010, we devoted a lengthy chapter to comparing the development of the women's game in Europe and the United States. Our main finding was that women on both continents engaged in pioneering work though in differing contexts. Whereas the Americans entered a field that was largely empty of men mainly because the sport itself was culturally marginal; the Europeans had to work their way onto a field totally dominated by men. The American women proceeded to excel at a game in which men in America were mediocre producers and marginal consumers thereby becoming trailblazers in soccer's massive growth and success in American culture. The European women have come to redefine however slowly but stoutly football's male domination in Europe. American women became de novo and even ex nihilo major architects of soccer in the United States whereas European women came to re-arrange an already existent edifice. Both achievements have been immensely taxing but also massively beneficial for the overall being of Association Football. Interior decorators and landscape designers are every bit as important to the overall quality of life and habitat as are foundational engineers. And the construction project is far from over. The struggle continues. This little book is an updated and much expanded version of my chapter in *Gaming the World*. As such, it stands for my continued homage and respect to women soccer players in America and women footballers in Europe, cultural trailblazers on both sides of the Atlantic regardless of what nomenclature one uses to identify them.

****

I would like to thank Grant Wahl most kindly for encouraging me to rework my chapter from *Gaming the World* and write this book. I would never have done so on my own. I owe deep gratitude to Jackson Bunis whose helping hand as my stellar research assistant proved indispensable for the completion of this work. Lastly, without my friend and colleague Fred Amrine's expertise in all things book publishing on Amazon and his wonderful hands-on support throughout this process, this book would never have happened.

I dedicate this book to my beloved wife Kiki and to all our golden retrievers who have enriched our lives so immeasurably over the past thirty-five years: Jascha, Dovi, Kelly, Stormi, Cleo Rose, Cody and Emma.

I also dedicate this book to the memory of my dear friend, professorial colleague and academic co-author Christopher S. Allen with whom I spent many hours watching soccer live and on television, from the New England Tea Men and the Boston Breakers to Manchester United and Real Madrid; from MLS Cup finals to many World Cup matches, both male and female. Chris became a committed pioneer in the world of American soccer fandom in the late 1970s and early 1980s when such was still a rare and uphill endeavor. He was a stout member of Sam's Army in the 1990s some of whom, I am sure, remember him with fondness like I do.

INTRODUCTION

Frequently the conventional term 'feminization' of a profession not only entails the increased presence of women in it but sometimes the concomitant departure of men from it, thus occasionally leading to its putative diminished prestige and status. Thus, in the case of all sports, the increased entrance and participation of women is nothing short of revolutionary since the early 1970s. Just think of women's boxing becoming a medal sport at the 2012 Olympics, with wrestling being an old-timer. Or the fact that at the summer Olympics in Rio de Janeiro in 2016, the United States' team for the first time in its history featured more female than male athletes. I doubt, however, that this development of massively increased participation by women has led to a diminution of the prestige and status of men sports even though oddly the fear of such a loss in prestige and status is pervasive among men. Indeed, many men resent what they perceive as women's encroachment on what men (re)guard as one of their last uncontested domains linking aspects of their preferred sports' modernization and their increased "cosmopolitanization" with an unwanted and disdained "feminization" of them. Indeed, frequently one of the common defensive derisions directed against newcomers in an established sport or the arrival of a new sport in a country's established sport space centers on their alleged femininity and their feminized undermining of manly traditions that lend the established sports their real authenticity.

The revolutionary influx of women into the world of sports pertains mainly to performing and producing them; however, in terms of "speaking" sports – meaning the valorizing of sports as an all-encompassing quotidian aspect of one's life -- the traditional gender divide remains immense with the consumption of sports as an essential ingredient of everyday life still largely a male domain.[1] After all, the essence of manliness remains an absolute core to the self-esteem of many a sport, certainly all comprising those sports followed by millions on a daily basis, something I have come to call "hegemonic sports culture". In an earlier work, I defined "hegemonic sports culture" as that pervasive construct which is defined not by a sport's being played or performed – i.e. its production – but by its being following – i.e. its consumption. It is thus understood to be the "watching, following, worrying, debating, living and speaking a sport rather than merely playing it."[2] While there is a nexus between "doing" and "following" a sport, the distinct characteristic of a sport constituting "hegemonic sports culture" is that one need never have played it on any level and yet follow it and its teams and protagonists with an all-consuming passion as well

---

[1] Andrei S. Markovits and Emily Albertson, Sportista: *Female Fandom in the United States* (Philadelphia: Temple University Press, 2012). In an empirical study of women sports fans utilized by Markovits and Albertson in *Sportista*, Gillian Lee Warmfalsh demonstrates powerfully how women "speak" i.e. consume sports differently than men. See Gillian Lee Warmflash, *In a Different Language: Female Sports Fans in America* (Senior Honors Thesis, The Committee on Degrees in Social Studies, Harvard University, 2004). This is corroborated in a study of men and women among athletes and non-athletes at the University of Michigan. Indeed, the gender gap proved greater than the difference between athletes and non-athletes in terms of the respective knowledge and usage of sports languages. See Andrei S. Markovits & David T. Smith, "Sports Culture among Undergraduates: A Study of Student-Athletes and Students at the University of Michigan," *The Michigan Journal of Political Science* 2: 9 (Spring 2008), pp.5-58.
[2] Andrei S. Markovits and Lars Rensmann, *Gaming the World: How Sports Are Reshaping Global Politics and Culture* (Princeton: Princeton University Press, 2010); p. 13.

as a great sophistication in knowledge and expertise. One need never have hit a baseball in New England to be a rabid Boston Red Sox fan, nor did one ever have kicked a soccer ball in the Boca district of Buenos Aires to experience undying love of Boca Juniors akin to a religious devotion. Playing and following are two distinctly different social phenomena in the world of sports. Bottom line: Soccer's feminized presence is a newcomer to Europe and America. Because of the game's different standing in the two continents' respective hegemonic sports cultures the concrete nature of this feminization assumes distinctly different characteristics in the European and American contexts.

The words "women" and "soccer" make a natural pairing in American English. They roll off the tongue easily, they make sense, they are not contradictory, they need little, if any, explanation or qualification. They are compatible, congruent, and even harmonious with each other. The term "soccer mom" has not only entered the American vernacular but as such it clearly constitutes a widely recognizable sociological category. Everybody knows what it denotes: a middle-aged white woman living in the suburbs, well-educated with a post-graduate degree, working at a minimum in a position of middle-management often indeed much higher than that, driving a minivan which she deploys regularly for transporting her children and their cohort to violin lessons and soccer games. Contrast this situation to the lexical dyad of "women" and "football". This pairing is still somewhat incompatible and invokes tension, alienation, antagonism, and even estrangement. The term "football mum" in British English, does not really exist. It most definitely does not come anywhere close to having the cultural presence that "soccer mom" has in North America. And were "football mum" in frequent usage in Britain, it most certainly would connote something completely different in its social signification than does "soccer mom".

I will analyze how the very fact that this game is called "soccer" in the United States constitutes an exceptional situation that renders its symbiosis with women smooth, and even "natural". The term "soccer" denotes a subordinate status because the term "football" has been accorded to the predominant code in each society in which a related game of close affinity received cultural pride of place over the past century. Fittingly, women in the United States have remained virtually excluded as players in the world of (American) football and continue to be subordinate to every facet of this sport's existence with the possible exception of cheerleading.[3] Lastly, I will highlight how women in Europe had actually entered the world of their football around World War I but how they remained marginal to it to this day. As we will soon see, though, significant shifts have happened in the course of the past 40 years on both continents.

---

[3] I know, of course, that there exist women's football teams and leagues in the United States. And I also know that the occasional young woman has assumed an important role on a high school's or even Division Three colleges' squad, but – tellingly – always as a kicker, arguably the least valued and most ridiculed position in American football. "Real" football players often do not regard kickers as "real" players but as sissies, foreigners – in short not as "real" men and as part of the game's "real" core.

Women and soccer, as well as women and football – different as these pairings may be – have one essential common denominator. They form an integral part of what constitutes in my mind one of the major stories of the second wave of feminism, namely the massive advance of women as sports producers – i.e. as players – that has almost attained the level of men. All this has happened in the course of the past 40-odd years and is most definitely a direct consequence of the revolutionary impact in the United States of Title IX passed in 1972. As *The New York Times* wrote in an article on June 16, 2012: "It's hard to exaggerate the far-reaching effect of Title IX on American society. The year before Title IX was enacted, there were about 310,000 girls and women in America playing high school and college sports; today, there are more than 3,373,000." This constitutes an amazing statement and bespeaks a massive shift in gender relations. Consider this: At my own University of Michigan, there were for all intents and purposes as late as the early 1970s no female varsity athletes. Most certainly, women were all but nonexistent in the University's team sports. The University of Michigan, as of 2018, features 29 varsity teams, 15 of which were for women and 14 of which were for men. In terms of the numbers of student athletes, however men's teams, with 485 total members, exceed the women's, with 375, by over 100 student athletes. Women compete vigorously in team sports such as basketball, volleyball, softball, soccer and field hockey to name but a few. There still is no complete gender equality since women play softball a "female" version of baseball that men do not play on the varsity level. Moreover, women do not play football at Michigan, or any other college or university, confirming yet again the aforementioned culturally constructed incompatibility between women and football in America. Moreover, women's massive entry into sports since the 1970s remains largely confined to the world of sports production — the "doing" of sports, the participating and performing in them — rather than in their consumption — the "following" of sports, the knowledge of sport history and details, and the all-encompassing identification with them to the point of a singular passion bordering on obsession. Still, women's entrance into the world of sports production is a global phenomenon that marks a significant cultural shift in gender relations on a global level.

I argue that this shift is nowhere more powerfully manifested than in the world of soccer in America and football in Europe and the rest of the world. For reasons that are far too complex to be presented satisfactorily in this venue, soccer in the United States played a subordinate role in American sports culture – as well as general culture – throughout the 20th century. While there were clearly certain epochs in which soccer was indeed very popular in the United States and could potentially have rivaled – perhaps even surpassed – football's and basketball's (though not baseball's and boxing's) cultural presence in the 1920s, for example[4]; it would not be inappropriate to characterize the presence of soccer's cultural proliferation as of the late 1970s and early 1980s as "olympianized" meaning that the sport developed a certain quadrennial cultural awareness and popularity during the World Cup – and later even the EURO – tournaments not dissimilar to that of the Olympics.[5] And our supporting sports during the Olympics and the World Cups has everything to do with Jerry Seinfeld's brilliant dictum about what, in essence, we are really supporting with our rooting passion and interest in all sports: laundry! (i.e. the "USA" on the athletes' uniforms for Americans and the equivalent country name for fans in that nation). Essentially, we know next to nothing about the sports whose athletes we exhort to win. Rather, our very temporary passion rests on our identifying them as Americans, hence we cheer for them quadrennially at World Cups and Olympic Games. However, in both cases – Olympics and World Cup -- the sports practiced between these mega events have largely remained confined to the periphery of the American sports scene. Few people beside the actual athletes, their fans and the sport's aficionados care about virtually any Olympic disciplines on a daily level. Ditto with soccer in the United States – until recently!

---

[4] It is very clear that had the American Soccer League (ASL) not succumbed to the internecine battles between league and federation starting in 1928, this league had the potential to place soccer in America on the country's cultural map. After all, the ASL surpassed the fledgling NFL in attendance and popularity at the time. On this subject, see Brian Phillips, "The Secret History of American Soccer" in *Slate* posted on June 9, 2010. But above all, David Wangerin, *Soccer in a Football World* (Philadelphia: Temple University Press, 2008); and Colin Jose, *American Soccer League: 1921 – 1931: The Golden Years of American Soccer* (Lanham, Maryland: Scarecrow Press, 1998)

[5] I have done some work on soccer's "Olympianization" in my previous work on sports. See Andrei S. Markovits and Steven L. Hellerman, "The 'Olympianization' of Soccer in the United States" in <u>American Behavioral Scientist</u>, Volume 46, Number 11 (July 2003); pp. 1533 - 1549.

In the American case, women contributed immensely to the change in soccer's cultural position on the firmament of American sports. One could almost see them as the vanguard in this change certainly by dint of their amassing trophies and medals which, surely, remain the most essential measuring sticks of any protagonist's success in this endeavor. I would go so far as to argue that women in the United States became integral, even indispensable, forces in the building of this sport's current existence in America. One simply cannot write a book on American soccer without according women pride of place and a central role.

In the United States, women stepped into the world of soccer that was marginal at best and they managed to construct a level of excellence in it in two decades—from the early 1970s until the early 1990s with their winning the first FIFA-sanctioned Women's World Cup in 1991 -- that really has few parallels in any sport practiced by either gender. By dint of their phenomenal successes and unique achievements, the American female soccer players catapulted a formerly obscure and unimportant sport on America's cultural periphery if not quite into the center of American sports culture then most certainly into a respectable space within it. The achievement of American women players was not so much to overcome male resistance to their entering a hitherto sacred male turf since soccer mattered little to American males. Instead, American women proved to be pioneers in blazing the way for a hitherto little-known and ill-respected sport in America's sports culture and sports space.

In contrast, one could, in fact, write a book on the history of European football in which women were accorded a rather marginal presence. The centrally pioneering feat of European women consisted in their daring to enter a realm and play a game that was – and still is – arguably the most male-centered sector of European public life (excepting, perhaps, the Catholic Church). If the achievement of American female soccer players was to help legitimate a sport, their European sisters' accomplishment was crashing the gates of an exclusively male club. Even though, as we will see in the next section, women's soccer existed in Europe since the early 1900s, most certainly since after World War I, these precursors to today's women's football in Europe were virtually irrelevant to the contemporary scene excepting perhaps the keen interest of historians. The phenomenon that commenced with the late 1960s and really emerged in the 1970s and 1980s had virtually nothing to do with its meek and obscure precursors of the early part of the 20th century. Instead, the recent and current impressive accomplishments had everything to do with the second wave of feminism and a concomitant rethinking and re-prioritizing of many aspects of social and cultural discourse in the West best known by the term "culture turn". Probably no female European soccer player of the 1970s and 1980s knew of or cared about female players in the 1920s or before. Rather, the new generation's motivations, commitment and passion for the game, and its courage to challenge this male bastion — despite repeated and constant male ridicule and hostility — emanated from the changed position and discourse surrounding women in the advanced industrial countries of what could broadly be called "the West", i.e. member countries of the Organization for Economic Cooperation and Development (OECD). So even though the worlds of American soccer and European football were massively different in the late 1960s, the 1970s and the 1980s, the worlds of the two continents' respective women's movements and changed public discourse about gender and women were very similar, if not identical.

Excepting the World Cup tournaments which have become huge global events in the course of the past twenty years, women's soccer in America and women's football in Europe continue to remain peripheral cultural phenomena and marginal occurrences in terms of the topography of the respective hegemonic sports cultures on the two continents. Even the World Cup in the women's game remains subordinate to other, often culturally more marginal, events. A quick Google search on Google.com (Google in the United States) for "World Cup 2015" which was the most recent Women's World Cup, features first the Cricket World Cup followed by the Rugby World Cup – both also played in 2015 -- with the Women's World Cup coming in third even in the United States (never mind Britain and the Commonwealth countries) where cricket and rugby are culturally much more marginal than soccer. Still, women play this game in growing numbers in every advanced industrial country, and there is every indication that this will, if anything, increase in years to come. Just look at its spread in countries of Latin America, Africa and Asia. Maybe someday women and football in Europe and the rest of the world will become as compatible as women and soccer have been in the United States and American English since the beginning of the early 1970s.

This book's structure will proceed as follows: In Chapter One, I will briefly discuss the women's game in the era preceding the second wave of feminism. The next two chapters will present the world influenced and shaped by this second wave. Chapter Two will feature a presentation of the developments in Western Europe in which I will feature England, Germany and the Scandinavian countries of Denmark, Sweden and Norway. Chapter Three, comprising a few lengthy segments, will present women's soccer's development in the United States. A brief conclusion will end this work.

CHAPTER ONE:

The History of Women's Soccer until the Second Wave of Feminism

Women playing Association Football is not a new phenomenon at all. Indeed, there is strong historical evidence that in some European countries women basically began to play this game soon after men did or in some cases played alongside them both temporally and spatially. There have been accounts of women playing on the grass roots level like village greens and heaths and meadows in the 1860s and 1870s. The first recorded women's football match in the British Isles hails from 1888 in Inverness, Scotland. This was exactly the same year in which the men's game saw the establishment of the very first professional soccer league in England thus the world. It was also precisely 25 years after the founding of the Football Association in 1863 and some fifty years after the game's disparate origins germinated in the exclusive world of upper-class English boys and their public schools as well as the colleges of Cambridge University. "This [match] can be interpreted as distinct from folk football, like the late eighteenth-century women's games, or mixed holiday games such as the Shrove Tuesday free-for-all in the English town of Atherstone, though it did pit the married against the single women. In the Inverness game, the two teams had uniforms, fixed goals, a fairly stable and even number of members and the game had a limited time span,"[6] all essential ingredients of the modern game of football. A match pursuant to the guidelines of the Scottish Football Association was played on Shawfields Ground in Glasgow in 1892.[7] By 1895, the appropriately named Nettie Honeyball, secretary of the British Ladies, organized the English North versus South game at Crouch End in London to be followed by games in the Midlands, the North and in Scotland, "the most significant of which was the Newcastle fixture with a crowd approaching 8,000."[8] From its very beginning, the game became an integral part of sensitive conflicts involving class and gender in England, Scotland and the European continent at the time. Were these females playing the game "ladies" or "women"? Was football the proper pursuit for a girl from a bourgeois home or did this activity not behoove her station? Whatever the specifics of these socially fraught phenomena might have been, women playing the game must have caused sufficient commotion and worries for the Football Association to issue a ruling as early as 1902 preventing men's clubs from playing against "lady teams".[9]

In Germany, there are some records from 1900 of young girls kicking a ball to each other in a circle.[10] This was the year when the German Football federation, the Deutscher Fußball-Bund (DFB) was established though the men's game was nowhere near as popular at the

---

[6] Jean Williams, "The Fastest Growing Sport? Women's Football in England" in Fan Hong and J.A. Mangan (eds.) *Soccer, Women, Sexual Liberation: Kicking Off a New Era* (London: Cass, 2004), p. 113.
[7] Ibid.
[8] Ibid.
[9] Ibid.
[10] Beate Fechtig, *Frauen und Fußball* (Ebersbach: Edition Ebersbach, 1995), p. 11.

time as it was in England. Still, even at this nascent stage, young women played the game in an environment that engaged in a debate as to whether girls should be permitted any physical activities at all and whether such involvement might be either detrimental to their bodies (chiefly their reproductive capabilities) or just inappropriate behavior for a woman. There raged controversy at this time whether women were even allowed to participate in gym classes at school. From the very beginning, women interested in playing football had to overcome the extant male prejudice of this activity being unseemly and unhealthy for women. The latter view has certainly abated in the course of the last 30-40 years. As to the former, while things have most definitely improved, there still exists a strong male (and even female) perception in countries where football constitutes hegemonic sports culture that women who play this game are either unfeminine in their very being or are – at a minimum – engaging in an activity that should remain a man's domain.

In Sweden, Denmark, Norway, Belgium and France women began to play football in the early years of the 20th century in a disorganized and rudimentary manner. But just like in Germany, these remained much less prominent than in the British Isles for obvious reasons; the men's game, too, was at this time much less well anchored and institutionalized on the continent than in Britain, the modern game's original home. This was to change massively in the course of World War I. Even in the world of football – both on the men's and the women's side – the Great

War brought great changes as it did in numerous other facets of life. Many of these changes solidified a hugely enhanced popular participation that most certainly introduced women in the public realm like never before with nothing being more important than granting them the right to vote. These changes heralded a breakdown of the old order in virtually all aspects of public life, from politics to economics, from social mores to culture with women being important agents in all of them. It was in the immediate pre- and post-World War I era that men's football really prospered on the European continent and became the hegemonic sports culture that we have come to know throughout the 20th century, thus replicating its well-ensconced presence on the Continent that the game had enjoyed in England before the Great War. World War I also formed a watershed in the women's game. In 1917, the first women's football championships were held in France and in 1922 two football cup competitions were introduced.[11] In Sweden, the first women's football team was established in 1917. Its initial opponents were old-boys' sides. One of these matches attracted 1,700 spectators. The first match between two women's teams occurred in Stockholm in front of approximately 500 spectators.[12] Women played men in Kristiania (now Oslo) in 1919 and continued doing so on a regular basis throughout the 1920s.[13] Though much behind the Scandinavian countries

[11] Gertrud Pfister, "The Challenges of Women's Football in East and West Germany: A Comparative Study" in Fan Hong and J.A. Mangan (eds.) *Soccer, Women, Sexual Liberation: Kicking off a New Era* (London: Cass, 2004), p. 131.
[12] Jonny Hjelm and Eva Olofsson, "A Breakthrough: Women's Football in Sweden" in Fan Hong and J.A. Mangan, (eds.) *Soccer, Women, Sexual Liberation*, p. 182.

and Britain, Germany and Austria experienced the formation of a few female football clubs. As the scholarly authorities on these two countries emphatically tell us, though, these attempts should in no way be construed as full-fledged steps towards the introduction of the women's game. In both countries there was decided resistance to have the "fairer sex" engage in any kind of male sport, particularly football.[14]

The immediate post-World War I era witnessed the blossoming of the women's game in England. Similar to the female baseball leagues in the United States during World War II as depicted in the well-known movie "A League of Their Own", when women were granted a sudden temporarily vacated space to showcase their sport with so many men at war, in England, too, women's football teams proliferated all over the country during the Great War. By 1921, there were 150 women's teams playing matches on regular schedules. Two teams deserve mention here: Bennets' of London and Dick, Kerr's of Lancashire.[15] During World War I, female workers of the Dick, Kerr Munitions and Engineering Works factory in Preston, Lancashire, joined apprentices who comprised the company team for football matches during lunch and tea time.[16] One

---

[13] Kari Fasting, "Small Country – Big Results: Women's Football in Norway" in Fan Hong and J.A. Mangan (eds.) *soccer, Women, Sexual Liberation*, p. 150.

[14] For Germany, see the previously book by Beate Fechtig. For Austria, see Rosa Diketmüller, "Frauenfußball – Ein Paradigmenwechsel?" in Eva Kreisky and Georg Spitaler (eds.) *Arena der Männlichkeit: Über das Verhältnis von Fußball und Geschlecht* (Frankfurt: Campus, 2006), 347- 365.

[15] Jean Williams, "The Fastest Growing Sport?" p. 115.

[16] I owe this information, as well as all subsequent mention of the Dick, Kerr Ladies to the pioneering work of David Litterer, one of America's foremost soccer historians. The piece from which I garnered this information is entitled "Overview of Women's Soccer in the USA" and was shared with me via an e-mail attachment on Tuesday, January 22, 2002. An updated version appeared in 2005 under the slightly revised title "Women's Soccer History in the

day in October 1917, a stretch during which the company team was not very successful, some of the female players boasted that they could play the game better than the men. This led to a challenge by men to play the women. The match was held and duly reported in the press, but the score was never revealed. This constituted the beginning of the Dick, Kerr Ladies, arguably the best-known female football team until the modern era starting in the early 1970s. Indeed, this team continued to play for nearly fifty years. On Boxing Day in 1920, the Dick, Kerr Ladies played another team from Lancashire called the St. Helen's Ladies before a crowd of 53,000 at Goodison Park in Liverpool, the hallowed home ground of the pedigreed English football club Everton. Apparently, there were another 10 to 15,000 fans locked out of the completely packed stadium. Maybe it was this event, coupled with other signs of the growing popularity of the women's game in England, which mobilized the Football Association to ban all female competition from its grounds, in effect killing the women's game in its nascent stage. It would not be the first and last time that men stymied burgeoning developments in women's organizational initiatives which men perceived as threatening. Ironically, this ban was not lifted until 1970, the very year that the Dick, Kerr Ladies finally folded as a team.

The Dick, Kerr Ladies not only played an absolutely key role in the early phase of women's football in Britain, but also in that of

---

USA: An Overview" at the following link: http://www.rsssf.com/usadave/am-soc-overview-wom.html.

women's soccer – and soccer as a whole -- in the United States. The team toured the United States in 1922. After having been snubbed by the Canadian association, the team arrived in the United States to find that there were no established women's teams for it to oppose. If anything, women's soccer in the United States was even less developed at this stage than was football in Britain and Europe. Women's soccer – if it existed at all – was at best confined to gym classes, informal pick-up games and intramural competition at colleges, places where the game continued its meager existence until it burst onto the American sports scene with a vengeance beginning in the early 1970s and truly proliferating throughout the 1980s and 1990s. The Dick, Kerr Ladies were thus compelled to play men's teams. They opened with a 6 – 3 loss to Paterson F.C., but drew with J&P Coates, and the Fall River Marksmen (the team of legendary male American players like Bert Patenaude, the first soccer player anywhere in the world to score a hat trick at a World Cup which happened in a U.S. game against Paraguay in the first World Cup in Uruguay in 1930 where the American men, incidentally, still attained their most advanced position in this tournament by reaching the semifinals; and, of course, Billy Gonsalves, the Babe Ruth of American soccer) , and defeated the New Bedford Whalers. Both of these teams belonged to the professional American Soccer League, which – at the time – featured some superb players on a global scale and sported teams that could – and did – hold their own against fine British and European sides. Overall, the Dick, Kerr Ladies' tour record was 3 wins, 2 ties or draws, and 2 losses, surely an impressive feat, although – as David Litterer informs us, "the men's sides were sometimes going easy on the Ladies, much to their chagrin."[17] The Dick, Kerr Ladies' overall record during their 48-year existence was 758-46-24, an impressive mark by any standards. Their pioneering trail for women's football in Britain and Europe, and women's soccer in the United States, deserves much greater attention than it has hitherto received on either side of the Atlantic.

Suffice it to say that the women's game which seemed to flourish, albeit still on a very meager level, compared to the amazing boom experienced by the men's in the 1920s and 1930s, was all but banned and officially stymied in many European countries. In some countries, there ensued official bans (e.g. in Austria in 1936) which prohibited women, like in the aforementioned decision by the English Football Association of 1921, to play on any grounds that were under the jurisdiction of the national associations and federations. In effect, women were barred from playing football in any public and official manner. While in Germany the Nazis did not need such an official decree to ban the women's game -- and it was not until 1955 that the Deutscher Fußball-Bund (DFB) officially forbade the game on any of its grounds -- women's football completely disappeared in the Germany of

---

[17] Ibid.

the 1930s and 1940s. No such official prohibitions were needed in the Scandinavian countries and in France to have the game all but disappear in the course of the late 1920s and 1930s.

The question of whether the football establishments in these countries stymied the women's game because they actively feared it as a serious competition to the men's game, or whether these outright prohibitions and unofficial suppressions occurred for other reasons, reaches beyond the purview of my project here. Nevertheless, the women's game would not reappear in any meaningful way until the late 1960s and early 1970s, the beginning of the second wave of feminism, which – not coincidentally – overlapped considerably with a rising cosmopolitan discourse and one that has enhanced both empathy and compassion as an important ingredient in social and political life on both sides of the Atlantic. Above all, this second wave of feminism spawned a massive wave of inclusion of the formerly excluded way beyond women and has to thus be regarded as one of the most potent democratizing agents in the history of liberal democratic regimes in advanced capitalism. The integrative movements of the past 40 years, among which the second women's movement has assumed pride of place, have facilitated the changing position of women in soccer in the United States and football in Europe to a discussion of which I now turn.

CHAPTER TWO:

From Freaks and Unwelcome Intruders to a World of Marginalized Normalcy: Women's Football in Europe from the late 1960s until the Present

Introduction

As was the case in many a social and cultural, though not political, instance, in the world of women's soccer, too, the Great War proved a more potent force for change than did World War II. Even during the former, but most certainly right after it, women commenced to play the game in a few European countries in a somewhat organized fashion. Let us not forget that this coincided with women's entering the public sphere in the countries of advanced capitalism like they never did before. Far and away the most significant manifestation of this development was, of course, as already mentioned, women's acquisition of the franchise (the right to vote) which meant that at least nominally and in a formal manner, women had attained a voice in politics and the public that – with very few exceptions like Norway and New Zealand -- they simply did not have before. And it was precisely this nascent but discernable challenge to male hegemony in politics but also, of course, in sports and culture, that compelled the national soccer establishments everywhere to roll back the women's game, thus all but ending it.

No similar developments appeared during and after World War II. Women in Europe did not play football during the war and did not pick up the game after it either. Indeed, if anything, the German Federation's official banning of the game in 1955 underlined yet again how much the postwar restoration of the 1950s attempted to protect and solidify the gender status quo way beyond football. However, this blissful era of unprecedented consumption and the alleged "end of ideology" was to reach a permanent demise during the turbulent 1960s. Twenty years after the end of World War II, following a delayed reaction as it were, a cultural shift and social upheaval was to rock the West's bourgeois order, in essence ending many of its key codes that were its anchor arguably from the post-Napoleonic era though certainly since Victorianism. The history of women's football since then bespeaks some of these massive cultural and social changes. I will first present the developments in a few European countries before, in the next chapter, we will traverse the Atlantic Ocean and conclude this work with a detailed account of women's soccer in the United States.

England

Tellingly, it was in 1969 that the English Women's Football Association (WFA) was officially formed with 44 affiliated teams. One year later, the Football Association (FA) lifted its ban that had kept women from its grounds for nearly half a century. The number of clubs in the WFA grew consistently on an annual basis to the point that by 1996 the teams were divided into women's teams (comprising 600) and girls' teams (750). By 2000, there were 700 registered women's teams with the girls' teams holding steady at 750. In terms of registered players, none were tallied until 1979 when the first such statistic appeared with 6,000 registered female players in England. By 2000, this had ballooned to 35,000.[18] Indeed, the WFA's success in fostering women's football in England since the late 1960s could – paradoxically – best be gauged by the fact that as of 1992 the Football Association itself assumed all responsibilities of women's football in England. Rather than an outright usurpation by the FA of the WFA, this development represented the latter's alignment with the structures of the former. Thus, for example, the WFA had inaugurated a national football league in England in 1991 which was modeled on its male counterpart and furnished the very first such permanent structure in women's football in England.

---

[18] Jean Williams, "The Fastest Growing Sport," p. 123.

The era of the 1980s and the first half of the 1990s was dominated by the Doncaster Belles who won the FA Cup six times after reaching the final 11 times. The squad also won the first women's league title in 1992 and was crowned league champion once again in 1994.

As of 1992-93, there exists an FA Women's Premier League in which 36 teams compete in three divisions very much akin to the pyramid format invented by English male football in 1888 and copied pretty much the world over (with the notable exception of the United States). There is the Women's Premier League National Division at the top with the Northern and Southern divisions running on an equal basis underneath this National Division. The winners of these leagues each season are promoted to the top-level National Division. The terms Women's Premiership and Ladies Premiership are generally used for the National Division only. Underneath the top-flight leagues are four Combination leagues – the South West, the South East, the Midland and the Northern Combinations. The Premiership's teams play – just like their male counterparts – for the league championship, the FA Cup, the League Cup and, since 1999-2000, the Community Shield. Arsenal were far and away the most successful side in English women's football over the game's first two decades with 9 league championships, 8 FA Cup victories, 8 League Cup triumphs and 5 victories in the Community Shield. Other teams with success have been Everton, Charlton Athletic, Millwall, Wimbledon, and Fulham, all well-established teams on the men's side. England's women's national team also made major strides in these first few decades. Improving from tournament to tournament, the English team, led by the Arsenal superstar Kelly Smith -- without any doubt a world-class player and among the very best of the women's game globally; subsequently an erudite commentator for Fox on that network's broadcasts of the Women's World Cup in Canada in 2015 -- held the heavily favored and superb German team to a $0 - 0$ tie/draw at the Women's World Cup in China in September 2007. Thus, the English women were the only team not to succumb to the formidable Germans, who went on to repeat as World Champions with the amazing feat of not losing to any opponent and without allowing even one goal throughout the entire tournament. The English women's side also held its own against a heavily favored American team for the first half of the game before eventually succumbing to the much more experienced Americans in the second half of the quarterfinal match by a score of $3 - 0$.

Despite these remarkable strides, women's football remains decidedly – and even officially – second class in England, arguably more so than in most other comparable advanced industrial democracies of Europe and North America. Soon after the ban on women's football was lifted, the Sex Discrimination Act of 1975 was drafted to "exempt football specifically and other contact competitive sports in general from gains in female equity, and this approach has been reinforced on more than one occasion and is still valid…Women have many other qualities superior to those of men, but they have not got the strength or stamina to run, to kick or tackle, and so forth."[19] Even though the legislation was repeatedly amended over its existence, the clause that limited female participation to competitive sports endured in its original form for decades.[20] However, the Act was finally repealed in its entirety in 2010, and replaced by the Equality Act of 2010 which officially alleviates any differences between men and women in terms of having access to any sport. But official law, as we all know, does not always correspond to actual behavior, belief and custom. Culturally and institutionally, women's football in England remains clearly a disadvantaged entity compared to the men's game.

While women in England have come to play football in a steadily increasing amount since the early 1970s, they still follow the game much less than men. In a survey conducted by the government in 1998 assessing the general living patterns of the British public, watching television and listening to music were at least eight times as popular as football for men and at least 80 times as popular as football for women.[21]

The story of the women's game in England replicates the old dilemma of the glass being half full or half empty. Clearly, with the baseline of the pre-1970s, the gains have been very impressive. But in any comparison with the men's game, the women's remains miniscule. To say that the Barclay's Premier League is hegemonic in England

---

[19] Ibid., p. 124.
[20] Ibid., p. 124.
[21] Ibid., p. 126.

would be a massive understatement. By many measures, this league has become far and away the most popular and most successful sports league in the world. There are only 20 teams each year that can boast the fact that their players are in the top tier of football in the country, and perhaps in the world. The players on these teams attain world renown and global stardom, but only in the male sphere of football. Women have struggled to earn a place on the field in England, let alone stardom in the country or world. Women's football has been growing in England though and one clear sign of this is that as of the 2017-2018 season, every club in the Premier League now fields both a men's and a women's team. Some Premier League teams have had a women's club for decades now, with Southampton having the oldest women's team among the current Barclay's Premier League teams having been founded in 1970.[22] This was circa 15 years before the remaining Premier League teams either founded or acquired existing women's teams. Most of the other EPL clubs created their women's teams between 1983-1989. Some clubs chose not to create their own teams, but rather acquire existing women's teams which they then brought under the control of the club. One example of this is Chelsea Football Club, an extremely successful men's club over the past two decades that would presumably possess the resources necessary to start its own women's team. Yet, it acquired a team that was known as the Chelsea Ladies Football Club in 2004

---

[22] https://www.southamptonwfc.co.uk/swfc-history

which, despite the affinity in names, had no connection to the men's side at all. In a way, this parallel existence of these two eponymous clubs is illustrative of the deep gender division that has permeated English football throughout its history. After all, the women's Chelsea Club had been founded in 1992 and thus was playing alongside the men's team for 12 years before the latter decided to acquire it with the men's side playing in front of millions of fans worldwide and to packed stadia every weekend all over England and the women's toiling away in virtually complete obscurity.[23]

One of the most surprising details in the story of women's football in England is that Manchester United, one of the globe's most successful and famous sports entities well beyond Association football and England's borders, did not have a women's team until the end of 2018. The leadership of Manchester United – the men's side -- applied for a women's team in March of 2018, with hopes that this team would be formed and admitted to the Women's Super League for the forthcoming season.[24] Once again this furnishes a fine example of the subordinate role of women's to men's football in England when a club of Manchester United's sheen, tradition, success and financial resources was the latest among the Premier League teams to field a women's side. One almost feels that this was done out of an ornery sense of obligation

---

[23] https://www.chelseafc.com/en/about-chelsea/chelsea-fc-women
[24] https://www.manutd.com/en/news/detail/club-statement-regarding-the-application-for-a-manchester-united-womens-team

to the changed tenor of the times rather than as an act of real conviction let alone passion.

Indeed, just because a Premier League club has a women's team, does not guarantee popularity with the club's existing fan base. When researching the women's clubs for this book, it was interesting to see how each of these established clubs presented their women's team to the world. Every website had a list of all the teams that were associated with the club (youth, academy and others), with many teams placing their respective women's team near the bottom of the list. The women's link not only followed the men's team, but frequently appeared behind – or below -- the academy team and possible prospects leading to the following typical sequence: men's team up top and center; followed by the academy teams, U-23, U-18; then the prospects; with the women's being last. This shows that at least these teams' management and web designers believe that many, if not most, of the teams' fans – indeed the outside world -- seem to care more about who could possibly be playing for the men's team in the future than they do about the women currently playing for their club. The quality of the women's websites is often much lower than that of the men's. The graphics are obsolete and appear not to be updated. Furthermore, every heading on the main club website, be it for the team's history, the team's legends, or any aspect related to the team, only has information pertaining to the men's team. There is little to no information listed for the women under these headings.

Moreover, whatever scarce information may be included about the women is relegated to the women's section of the website.

In order to better understand women's football in England, it is important to know about the league in which the women play, and the structure of that league. The women's league was originally called the Women's Premier League National Division (WPLND). It was founded in 1991. This league ran for roughly 20 years as the top league for women's football in England, with a maximum of 12 teams during any given season. In 2011, six teams left the WPLND in order to form the new league, which was called Women's Super League. The biggest change distinguishing this new league from its predecessor was that the new entity has been run from its very beginning by the Football Association, England's ultimate authority of football, including the EPL. The WPLND lasted for another three years after the WSL was created and served as the WSL's second tier. When the WSL started, there were only eight teams, but as of the 2017-2018 season, the top tier has expanded to 10 teams with 10 more in the second tier. There is also confirmation for the 2018-2019 season that the top tier of the WSL will feature 11 clubs.[25] The second tier of the WSL was created in 2014, three years after the league was first established. This expansion shows the amount of growth that women's football attained in a relatively short period of time. It was originally formed from the old Women's Premier

---

[25] https://www.bbc.com/sport/football/45355268

League National Division and was called the Women's Super League 2 but is now known as the FA Women's Championship. The top teams in the Championship can apply for promotion, but it is not guaranteed by dint of mere excellence and success on the field. Rather, the club must demonstrate that "all license criteria can be met"[26]. This shows that criteria related to matters off the pitch – such as fan attendance, financial standings etc. – are just as essential to promotion in the women's game as on-the-field success. The same is not true for relegation though, as the last placed team in the WSL will be demoted.[27] It seems that in the women's game teams exhibiting on-the-field failure need not demonstrate the standing of their licensing criteria as do successful teams to be permitted promotion. There are other smaller divisions under the FA Women's Championship, but they are not considered to be anywhere near the caliber of the WSL. Teams must succeed in these smaller divisions before applying for a license to enter the Championship.

It is interesting to note that most teams in the Women's Super League and Women's Championship are unaffiliated with Premier League clubs. As of the 2017-2018 season, only 8 of the 20 combined WSL and Championship teams had Premier League affiliations, while the remaining 12 were independent teams. Another interesting point about these teams is that nowadays an increasing number of clubs are

---

[26] http://dailycannon.com/2019/01/explained-wsl-champions-league-and-promotion-relegation-rules/

[27] Ibid.

choosing to call themselves "Women's teams" as opposed to "Ladies teams."[28] While EPL club affiliation might not seem important, it is worthy of mention that since the WSL's inception in 2011, only teams with affiliations to EPL men's teams have won the league: Liverpool, Arsenal, and Chelsea have all won the WSL twice, and Manchester City has captured one title. Chelsea and Manchester City have also been the runners-up twice in the league's history. Thus, one can safely assume that the resources provided by the Premier League clubs hold some benefits for the competitiveness of the WSL.

However, one benefit that decidedly does not carry over from the men's sport to the women's is the millions of fans who watch the men's matches over a season both as television viewers and stadium spectators. The WSL's season used to be during the summer but was recently changed to be a winter season sport, with matches starting in September and ending in May thus corresponding to the men's season. This change in season was meant to have the women's league mirror the men's playing time thus upgrading the women's game in yet another area. However, this change might have contributed to a negative consequence. While causation remains unclear, the switch of the women's calendar to correspond to the men's resulted in an 11% drop in average attendance for the women reducing the number to under 1,000 spectators per match.[29] Data from 2017-2018 show that the average attendance for EPL teams

---

[28] https://www.bbc.com/sport/football/45355268
[29] https://www.theguardian.com/football/blog/2018/oct/23/womens-football-gates-main-stadiums

ranged from 11,000 at AFC Bournemouth on the lowest end, to over 75,000 people per game for Manchester United on the highest.[30] No women's team in history has ever come close to those attendance figures for a regular season match. It is only when the championship matches are played that crowds rise to levels on par with middle of the pack men's attendance rates. The FA Women's Cup Final in 2017 had a reported audience of 43,000 people watching the game live at Wembley Stadium.[31] Not all the games can be played at Wembley however, and the grounds for women's games are located an average of 13 miles away from the main stadia used by the men's teams which leads to fans simply not being interested in travelling the extra time and distance in order to watch a women's game. This has led to a recent movement to have more women's games played in the clubs' main stadia.[32] The team leading this movement has been Manchester City.

In 2016, Manchester City was the only women's team to experience a growth in average crowd size, boasting a number of roughly 2,000 fans per game, while nearly every other team posted a decrease in average crowd size for that season.[33] Liverpool's men's team had an average spectatorship of just over 53,000 fans, while their women's team struggled to attain 700 people at the club's famed home ground of Anfield for its matches.[34] The WSL is aware of low

---

[30] https://www.statista.com/statistics/268576/clubs-of-the-english-premier-league-by-average-attendance/
[31] https://www.theguardian.com/football/blog/2018/oct/23/womens-football-gates-main-stadiums
[32] Ibid.
[33] Ibid.
[34] Ibid.

attendance for its games and has adjusted its standards for incoming teams. In order to apply for a license to enter the WSL or the Women's Championship for 2017, a team had to prove that it could attract an average crowd of at least 350 people, which is a miniscule number compared to the men's game. This number increased for the 2018 season where each club had to attain an average crowd size of 400 people.[35] The disparity here is telling of the gap between the male and female domains of this sport. It seems that the only time English people will watch and support women's football, is when the matches are being played for national pride. In this, the English behave like all other publics in the contemporary world. In England just like on the continent and in North America, women's football only attains fans' interest when it is performed by the national team with club games being stragglers in terms of attendance and interest.

Indeed, it is in the context of only two very specific events that female football players – the England national team in particular -- receive any recognition in England: The Olympic Games and the Women's World Cup. In this context, too, the situation in England conforms to that in all other comparable countries in advanced industrial democracies. The English team had its most successful run at the 2015 Women's World Cup in Canada. The English women played their way into the heart of the nation by fielding one of the most popular teams in

---

[35] The 2017/2018 Football Association Women's Super League– Competition Rules

the entire World Cup. In fact, the most attended game of the tournament was the quarter-final match between Canada and England, which featured a crowd of over 54,000 people.[36] Surely most of the fans were in the stadium in support of the Canadian home team. Still, the success of the English women did not go unnoticed by the footballing world, by the English public and most tellingly by the best of the country's male footballers who publicly acclaimed the women's successes at the tournament. Thus, for example, Manchester United and England superstar legend Wayne Rooney tweeted, "England women doing the country proud. Huge congratulations on reaching the semifinals."[37] The English women may well have advanced to the tournament's final had it not been for Laura Bassett's tragic own-goal in extra time thus having the England team fall to the more seasoned Japanese squad.

Most important, however, the England women's team's ultimate triumph was defeating the mighty Germans in the bronze medal game by the score of 1-0. Not only did the England women's team attain its very first soccer World Cup medal on this fateful Fourth of July in 2015, but the team succeeded in beating its German rivals for the very first time in 20 attempts. Better still, by attaining third place in the tournament -- behind the champion United States and the runner up Japan -- the England women reached a level of World Cup success that the men only accomplished once: in their famously winning the championship at

---

[36] https://www.fifa.com/womensworldcup/news/key-figures-from-the-fifa-women-s-world-cup-canada-2015tm-2661648
[37] https://twitter.com/waynerooney/status/614972195694116864?lang=en

home in England in 1966. At the tournaments in 1990 and 2018, the men came in fourth but left for home with no medal in each case. Lastly, let us not forget the importance as to whom the England women defeated: It was none other than Germany who, not only in the women's game, had become England's perennial historic nemesis and tormentor best characterized by England great Gary Lineker's famous saying that Football is a simple game: Twenty-two men chase a ball for 90 minutes and at the end, the Germans always win.

This third-place finish by the England team at the World Cup in Canada in 2015 automatically qualified the participation of a British team at the 2016 Olympics in Rio de Janeiro. This, however, was not to be since the respective football associations of Scotland, Wales and Northern Ireland would only consent to the creation of a British team had each of these separate football nations attained a qualification by itself. England's success was simply not enough. The power of this regional --indeed national -- pride is truly astounding bordering on the obstreperous and destructive since these associations preferred not to have their players participate at a major global event when they rightfully could have only because of their disdain for England. On this level of national parochialism, the women's game has come to mirror the men's passion for the local instead of the cosmopolitan.

Germany (with Pavel Brunssen)

By sheer coincidence in terms of the particular event at hand, yet anything but coincidental in the context of the rapidly changing discourse in Western liberal democracies and very much conforming with the beginning manifestations of the massive reforms wrought by the second wave of feminism in all liberal democratic countries of advanced capitalism, the Deutscher Fußball-Bund (DFB) – the all-powerful German Football Federation, the largest sports federation in the world – chose in 1970, like its English counterpart the Football Association, to recognize officially what it then tellingly called "Damenfußball" (ladies' football). The reason for the federation's change of mind rested in its worries of losing control of the women's football movement that had commenced to gather steam in the late 1960s. Behooving the DFB's position of being the uncontested monopoly lording over football's every aspect and competition level in Germany, the federation did not want to risk losing authority over an entity which its members and officials held in low esteem and on which they heaped nothing but contempt and ridicule.[38] The DFB did not want German women to play the game "in private" (meaning out of the federation's purview), but it also wanted to keep the women's game different from the men's.

---

[38] Beate Fechtig, *Frauen und Fußball*, pp. 31 – 36; and Gertrud Pfister, "The Challenges of Women's Football in East and West Germany: A Comparative Study", pp. 133, 134.

Women put pressure on the DFB from within Germany, whereby the development in other European countries – particularly the Scandinavian ones of Denmark, Sweden and Norway -- helped their cause during the late 1960s. Despite their exclusion from the male dominated football association, women in Germany continued playing football throughout the 1950s. They played in the streets and founded independent football clubs. German women participated in an international tournament in Berlin and shortly after played an international women's game in Stuttgart against the Netherlands in April 1958.[39] The 'Miracle of Berne' – the famous World Cup win by Germany's men's team on the Fourth of July in 1954 upsetting the heavily favored Hungarian team (the Magnificent Magyars also known as the "Golden Team") and in many ways having this victory fortify the postwar reconstruction and legitimation of the Federal Republic of Germany – was accompanied by enthusiasm for football by the German population as a whole. Thus, by dint of this victory, German women wanted not only to watch, but also to play football. This euphoria motivated the DFB's ban of women from football one year later. While a welcoming site on the one hand, such enthusiasm on the part of women was also perceived as threatening. The DFB legitimated its decision of 1955 by, among others, drawing on several 'medical' statements which

---

[39] Nadine Junker, *Frauen am Ball! Eine sozialwissenschaftliche Studie über die Motive bei den Protagonisten der Legalisierung des Frauenfußballs im DFB 1970* (Dissertation, Universität Duisburg-Essen, 2012), https://duepublico2.uni-due.de/servlets/MCRFileNodeServlet/duepublico_derivate_00033213/Junker_Diss.pdf, p. 99.

claimed that football would harm women's bodies and their health. The founding of independent women's football clubs in the 1950s was succeeded by the organization of practice camps in the 1960s which, in turn, spawned further interest in sport clubs by women after 1968, that magical year in the social and cultural development of so many western societies, Germany's included. These positive developments in the domestic context received important support from the international arena: The founding of the Federation of Independent European Female Football (FIEFF) in 1969 was undoubtedly an important contributing factor to the DFB's lifting its ban in 1970.[40] Additionally, the DFB's altering its stand must have also been influenced by the unofficial, that is not FIFA-sanctioned, World Cup in Italy organized by the FIEFF and played in July 1970. Due to the DFB's banning of women from playing football, no German national team competed in this tournament in Italy. However, despite the DFB ban, players of SC Bad Neuenahr participated in the contest though with no success. Still, their mere participation caused a public debate about the role of women in football in Germany. Only a few months later, the DFB finally permitted women's football and accepted it as a federation-sanctioned official activity.[41]

---

[40] Nadine Junker, *Frauen am Ball! Eine sozialwissenschaftliche Studie über die Motive bei den Protagonisten der Legalisierung des Frauenfußballs im DFB 1970* (Dissertation, Universität Duisburg-Essen, 2012), https://duepublico2.uni-due.de/servlets/MCRFileNodeServlet/duepublico_derivate_00033213/Junker_Diss.pdf, p. 104.

[41] Nadine Junker, *Frauen am Ball! Eine sozialwissenschaftliche Studie über die Motive bei den Protagonisten der Legalisierung des Frauenfußballs im DFB 1970* (Dissertation, Universität Duisburg-Essen, 2012), https://duepublico2.uni-due.de/servlets/MCRFileNodeServlet/duepublico_derivate_00033213/Junker_Diss.pdf, p.

Initially, the DFB decreed the women's game to last only 60 minutes instead of the 90 for the men's. The women's season would commence on the 1st of March and end on the 31st of October thus entail a "good weather" cycle as opposed to the men's that has traditionally commenced in late August or early September and has lasted until late May or early June with only a short respite during Christmas and New Year's.[42] Women were not to use typical football boots with studs on their soles but rather flat running shoes. Furthermore, due to the "female anatomy", no advertising was allowed on women's jerseys lest such attract the spectators' prurient attention and thus become a distraction from the game. Only females were permitted to coach women's teams and all players could only commence their season after having undergone a thorough medical examination by a specialist in sports medicine. Such an exam had to be repeated within four weeks after the completion of the season. Women were not allowed to use regular footballs but, instead, were required to play their games with so called "youth balls" which were lighter in weight and smaller in size. Lastly, women were not to play for a championship. Pursuant these special rules, the lifting of the prohibition of women's football did not in fact open football for women. Instead, it introduced "Frauenfußball" as a distinctly separate sport explicitly apart from the men's game.[43]

111f.

[42] The men's game in England has no provisions for even such a short break and continues uninterrupted from late summer to late spring.

[43] Simone Wörner & Nina Holsten, "Frauenfußball - zurück aus dem Abseits," *Aus Politik und Zeitgeschichte* (2011), http://www.bpb.de/apuz/33342/frauenfussball-zurueck-aus-dem-abseits?p=all.

But, "after initially modifying the rules to make them less 'rough' for women in the 1960s, the DFB then abandoned the modifications and gave official permission for women's matches to be played as double headers prior to men's professional matches. Thus, by May 1970 at an FC Kaiserslautern versus FC Cologne match [featuring two of German football's most pedigreed clubs, ASM], the Landau and Augsburg women's teams played in front of 18,000 people. Matches in the 1950s, 1960s and 1970s were often played as part of a town's Volksfest, annual people's fair, and filled town stadiums."[44]

Frankfurt proved to be an especially fertile ground for women's football as attested to by its current club 1. FFC Frankfurt that has developed into Germany's leading women's football club having won seven German league championships, a record nine German cups and four UEFA Champions League titles second only to the French side Olympique Lyonnais Feminin's five.

Although women played football in Frankfurt prior to the 1930s, the attempt by the only 19-year old Lotte Specht to establish women's football in 1930 was among the first that gained broader attention. In order to establish the 1. Deutsche Damenfußball Club Frankfurt, Specht searched for teammates via the newspaper *Frankfurter Nachrichten* and received approximately 40 responses. Despite weekly practice sessions

[44] Jean Williams, "Women's Football, Europe and Professionalization, 1971 – 2011", Research Report, International Centre for Sports History and Culture, De Montford University, 2012; p. 36. https://www.dora.dmu.ac.uk/bitstream/handle/2086/5806/Woman%27s%20football%2C%20Europe%20%26%20professionalization%201971-2011.pdf?sequence=1&isAllowed=y. This study was later published under the title *Globalising Women's Football: Europe, Migration and Professionalization* (Bern: Peter Lang, 2013).

and making it onto the title page of *Frankfurter Illustrierte* on 27th of March 1930, the team did not last long. Spectators not only hurled insults at the team, but also attacked the players with stones. Specht's requests for support were rejected by the DFB. After one year, the team folded. It took no less than 30 years until women's football in Frankfurt rose again.[45]

Some of the key teams in German women's football have been TuS Worrstadt (formed in 1969) who won the first national championship in 1974 and Bergisch Gladbach (formed in 1973) who won the national championship in 1977 and also the Cup Final in 1981 and 1982 and 1984. Bayern Munich, who won the national championship in 1976, were runners up in 1979. Bayern also came in second in the club's Cup Final appearances 1988 and 1990. We already mentioned the successes of 1. FFC Frankfurt (founded in 1998). "Before the reunification of Germany, 1. FFC Turbine Potsdam (fully known as '1. Frauen-Fußball-Club Turbine Potsdam 71 e.V') dominated the East German women's league. It remains the only team from the former East Germany to win the unified title. The team also won the UEFA women's competition in 2004/05 season, beating the Swedish team Djugarden/Alvsjo 5-1 overall in the final. Turbine Potsdam have been the most significant East German team to maintain a place in the Frauen

---

[45] Nadine Junker, *Frauen am Ball! Eine sozialwissenschaftliche Studie über die Motive bei den Protagonisten der Legalisierung des Frauenfußballs im DFB 1970* (Dissertation, Universität Duisburg-Essen, 2012), https://duepublico2.uni-due.de/servlets/MCRFileNodeServlet/duepublico_derivate_00033213/Junker_Diss.pdf, p. 65.

Bundesliga, created in 1990, after integration and the national team benefitted a great deal from East German players, in spite of the fact that the women had not been supported at all by the East German Football Association because football was not considered to be a top-level (i.e. Olympic) sport."[46] The German Democratic Republic's women's national team was founded only in 1990 at the tail end of the regime's existence. It played but one match before unification loosing 0:3 against a more experienced team from Czechoslovakia in front of 800 spectators on the 9th of May in Potsdam.

Telling of the rapidly changing times was the fact that by the 1972-73 season, most of these special rules for women just disappeared. All German states comprising the Federal Republic of Germany conducted championship rounds with home and away matches exactly like in the men's game; and the schedule soon became congruent with the men's in that the season commenced in the fall and ended in the spring. By the middle of the 1980s, women could – and did – play the game in football boots with cleats. The balls became identical to the men's. The only remaining female rule decreed by the DFB was the different length of the game, which in the course of the 1980s was expanded from the previous 60 minutes to 80 minutes. It was not until the early 1990s that the women's game became completely emancipated in that it shed all of

[46] Jean Williams, "Women's Football, Europe and Professionalization, 1971 – 2011", Research Report, International Centre for Sports History and Culture, De Montford University, 2012; pp. 36, 37. https://www.dora.dmu.ac.uk/bitstream/handle/2086/5806/Woman%27s%20football%2C%20Europe%20%26%20professionalization%201971-2011.pdf?sequence=1&isAllowed=y. This study was later published under the title *Globalising Women's Football: Europe, Migration and Professionalization* (Bern: Peter Lang, 2013).

its "female" specialties and exceptions by henceforth playing the 90 minutes that has constituted the duration of an Association football game throughout the 20th century. Women's football in Germany changed not only "from below", i.e. by dint of the ever-increasing number of young women flocking to the game, but also "from above" in that the Union of European Football Associations (UEFA) came to standardize the rules and regulations of the women's game on a continent-wide basis, eliminating the country- and even region-specific rules that guided women's football until then.

By 1971, there existed 1,110 women's teams in Germany. By 1982, this number had more than doubled and reached 2,891. Many of the players came to football from the game of field handball (an outdoors version of team handball that is played indoors on hardwood courts), then a very popular sport for men and women in Germany as well as some of the northern European countries like Sweden, Denmark and Norway. In 2018, there were 5,966 senior women's football teams and 5,346 female youth teams (under 17) furnishing a total of 11,312.[47] The increasing number of female members in the DFB since the 1970s is similarly impressive: In 1971, the DFB counted 39,534 female members but within ten years the number had multiplied tenfold to 383,171.[48] By 2001, the amount had almost doubled again to 630,082. Additionally,

---

[47] "DFB Mitglieder-Statistik 2018", https://www.dfb.de/fileadmin/_dfbdam/181845-DFB-Statistik_2018.pdf, p. 3
[48] Nadine Junker, *Frauen am Ball! Eine sozialwissenschaftliche Studie über die Motive bei den Protagonisten der Legalisierung des Frauenfußballs im DFB 1970* (Dissertation, Universität Duisburg-Essen, 2012), https://duepublico2.uni-due.de/servlets/MCRFileNodeServlet/duepublico_derivate_00033213/Junker_Diss.pdf, p. 118.

there were 211,734 female members under the age of 17.[49] Ten years later, when the women's World Cup was held in Germany, the number had increased to 720,407 (plus 338,583 under 17).[50] In 2018, the DFB counted 792,782 female members plus 313,322 players in its youth teams constituting a total of 1,106,104 women among the federation's total membership of 7,090,107 which amounts to 15,6%.[51] In contrast to the increasing number of women's teams, the number of men's teams decreased from 2017 to 2018.The increase of female members is just as impressive as the international success the German women footballers were able to accomplish. However, this has been neither echoed by their popularity, nor was this predictable in 1970, as we will show in the following paragraphs. Once again, as elsewhere, in Germany, too, there has existed a major discrepancy between women's football production and achievements on the field and its paucity in cultural acceptance and popularity off it.

1973 witnessed the first official women's football championship in Germany. It became institutionalized since then on a yearly basis. In addition to this annual championship, German women footballers – just like their male counterparts – also participate in a parallel cup competition. As of 1980, the individual winners of the 16 regions comprising the DFB compete in a play-off tournament for the DFB's

---

[49] "DFB Mitglieder-Statistik 2001", https://www.dfb.de/fileadmin/_dfbdam/25668-mitgliederstatistik_2001.pdf, p. 2.

[50] "DFB Mitglieder-Statistik 2011", https://www.dfb.de/fileadmin/_dfbdam/25662-DFB-Mitglieder-Statistik-2011.pdf., p. 2

[51] "DFB Mitglieder-Statistik 2018", https://www.dfb.de/fileadmin/_dfbdam/181845-DFB-Statistik_2018.pdf, p. 2.

women's National Cup whose winner then represents Germany's women's football national cup winner. The final game used to be played in Berlin's Olympic Stadium in early June as an opening act to the men's cup final. There was no better measure of the immense difference between the cultural perception and social presence of women's and men's football than this event which always featured two matches between two excellent women's and two excellent men's teams. The stadium was at best half full when the women started their game, with people streaming in for the impending men's game during the second half of the women's match. The mainly male crowd payed no attention to the women's game and often indulged in derision and lewd comments towards the women players on the field. Needless to say, while the ensuing men's match was played in a packed stadium and in front of millions of television viewers across Germany, the women's game never attracted anywhere close to a filled venue though it came to be aired on television during the 1990s and watched by a very small audience. Best denoting the respect that male football players – if most assuredly not male spectators and fans – came to accord their female counterparts was the fact that the players of the two men's teams that followed the women's match stopped commencing their warm ups right along the field's sidelines with the women's game still in full progress as happened well into the 1990s. Here, too, as has happened so often in all countries and contexts: athletes have accorded much more respect to fellow athletes than have spectators and fans! In Germany just like everywhere else, too, the sexism among male fans seems to exceed by far that among male players.

Yet another step in the gradual emancipation of women's football in Germany – at least on the formal and official level – was the decision to have the women's cup final decoupled from the men's in Berlin and played all in its own right and autonomously in Cologne starting in 2010. Although this decision was publicly praised in the euphoric context of the women's World Cup 2011 in Germany, it came with a price. Since 2010, there are, excepting track and field, no professional sporting events where women and men compete together in Germany. Arguably, this separation also contributes to the notion of two separate sports whereby women's football remains the marginalized exception from men's football which to many is still the only one that really counts and is worthy of the name. While the first women's cup final in Cologne attracted 26,282 spectators, the average attendance rate over the last years has decreased to 18,240 with an all-time low of 14,269 in 2017.[52] 17,692 spectators came to see Wolfsburg's cup win over Bayern Munich in 2018. In contrast, the men's final in Berlin attracted 74,322.

As of 1990, German women's football also has a regularized league championship. Teams were initially divided into 14 regional leagues and a national league with two divisions of 10 teams each with

---

[52] "Kampf um jeden Zuschauer" https://www.fr.de/sport/fussball/kampf-jeden-zuschauer-10991137.html, 19 May 2018.

the usual relegation and promotion so common to the men's game all over Europe and Latin America. But, as of the 1997-98 season, "12 teams have formed a national league with a single division in an attempt to concentrate women's football on the best clubs and thus raise standards of play."[53] Perhaps the most accurate gauge for the changed perception of this sport in the male establishment's eyes has been the fact that starting in the middle of the 1980s, it gradually came to be known and called "women's" as opposed to "ladies'" football ("Frauenfußball" instead of the former "Damenfußball"). However, this change did not diminish the special status ascribed to "Frauenfußball" opposed to men's football, which is always called simply "Fußball" and comes without a defining prefix. Gendered club names such as '1. Frauenfußballclub Turbine Potsdam 71 e. V. or '1. Frauen Fußball Club Frankfurt e.V.' are absolutely unthinkable in the men's game. This linguistic distinction echoes the separation between the norm and the exemption, the hierarchy between the hegemonic and the marginalized.

There is no better incident to exemplify the status of women's football as emancipated but still subordinate, than the belated two-fold celebrations of Wolfsburg's women's team in 2017. After winning the cup and the league in the same season (the famed "double") the city's men's club VfL Wolfsburg prohibited the women's team to celebrate – as already officially scheduled -- its great success of winning two

[53] Gertrud Pfister, "The Challenges of Women's Football in East and West Germany: A Comparative Study", p. 135.

coveted titles at Wolfsburg's city hall, because the men's team had to extend its season by two games in order to avoid relegation. In other words, women were not permitted to celebrate their successes if men still had to struggle for their existence in the country's top league. The men's club's decision was made despite the criticism of the women's team coach Ralf Kellermann who had learned about this decision only through the media.[54]

The language of hegemonic sports cultures remains masculine. Women's football is seen through a male gaze marginalized through strategies of separation and denigration.[55] The slogan of the Women's World Cup in 2011 linked women's football to the perception of the player's bodies: "20Elf von seiner schönsten Seite" ("2011 from its most beautiful side" also playing a pun on the date "eleven" and on "eleven" players comprising a football team). This slogan – not even using the terms "football" or "World Cup" – emphasized the male perspective on the women's game.[56] Two years earlier, the former player for Tennis Borussia Berlin and Turbine Potsdam Tanja Walther-Ahrens left the board of Berlin's football association in frustration regarding this matter. She explained her resignation as follows: "Women are still not taken

[54] "Wolfsburgs Meister-Frauen leiden unter dem Diktat der Männer", https://www.welt.de/sport/fussball/article164968347/Wolfsburgs-Meister-Frauen-leiden-unter-dem-Diktat-der-Maenner.html, 26 May 2017.
[55] Juliane Lang, 2015. "'Fußball' und 'Frauenfußball': Zum Blick des Fußballs auf seine 'jüngere Schwester'" Martin Endemann, Robert Claus, Gerd Dembowski, and Jonas Gabler (eds.) *Zurück am Tatort Stadion: Diskriminierung und Antidiskriminierung in Fußball-Fankulturen* (Göttingen: Die Werkstatt, 2015), p., p. 42.
[56] Simone Wörner & Nina Holsten, "Frauenfußball - zurück aus dem Abseits," *Aus Politik und Zeitgeschichte* (2011), http://www.bpb.de/apuz/33342/frauenfussball-zurueck-aus-dem-abseits?p=all.

seriously. Women's football is perceived as an appendage, as a bad version of men's football. But the eternal comparison to men's football harms women's football. One can only loose this comparison."[57]

Even before the women's World Cup tournament of 2011 began, five members of the junior German national team posed for the July issue of the German edition of *Playboy* with complete frontal nudity and in unambiguously sexualized depictions utilizing the requisite sexy lingerie and the ubiquitous stilettos.[58] The openly sexualized text accompanying these pictures was full of double entendre such as the ample usage of the word "Vorspiel" which in German means both preliminary rounds in a tournament as well as sexual foreplay.[59] Of course, words such as "ball" and "shot" and "run" and "play", among many others, appeared in describing innocuous soccer-related matters but always, of course, hinting at their all-too-obvious sexual meaning. The headline "We want to refute the clichés of the butch women" graced the interview section with the five women demonstrating that the issue of lesbians ruling German women's football, a widespread assumption on the part of the male-dominated soccer public, was a topic worthy of addressing (and commercializing) by *Playboy* and its models from the

---

[57] "Frauen werden im deutschen Fußball noch immer nicht ernst genommen. Frauenfußball gilt als Anhängsel, als schlechte Version des Männerfußballs. Doch der ewige Vergleich mit dem Männerfußball schadet den Frauen. Den kann man nur verlieren." Our translation. "Der ewige Vergleich mit dem Männerfußball schadet den Frauen", https://www.zeit.de/sport/2015-05/frauenfussball-dfb-tanja-walther-ahrens/komplettansicht, 14 May 2015.
[58] "WM-Vorspiel mit scharfen Schüssen" in *Playboy* (German edition), July 2011; pp. 29 – 42.
[59] I am greatly indebted to Temple University Press for so generously permitting me to use extensive parts of four pages from my book *Sportista: Female Fandom in the United States* co-authored with Emily Albertson and published by Temple University Press in 2012. The text used here hails from pages 97 to 100 in Sportista.

junior squad of the German women's national football team.[60] Indeed, the *Playboy* interviewer commenced one of his questions thusly: "In the 1970s and 1980s, there was allegedly not one single heterosexual player in Germany's national soccer team. How high is the percentage of lesbian players today?" To which one of the players, Ivana Rudelic, responded: "I was born in 1992 thus I was not even in planning in the 1970s and 1980s. And we have not conducted any scientific surveys thus far on the topic of the players' sexual orientation. Of course, there are homosexual players. That is no secret in women's soccer." And her teammate Julia Simic added the following insight depicting the massive difference between men and women in football (and all culturally hegemonic tam sports for that matter): "I think that there are some homosexual players among the men, too. But that issue remains a total taboo. And with good reason: Were such a player to reveal his sexual orientation and preference, he would have a terribly difficult life in the Bundesliga [Germany's top male professional soccer league]. With and for women, the issue is a lot less complicated."

In a fine research paper analyzing femininity and sexualization in women's soccer, Henrik Frach featured an in-depth interview with Kristina Gessat, one of the young soccer players posing on the cover of *Playboy,* to assess her conflicting position of a top-level athlete and budding national soccer star on the one hand, and a sex object on the

---

[60] "Wir wollen das Mannweiber-Klischee widerlegen" in Playboy (German edition), July 2011; pp. 44, 45.

other.[61] In addition to confirming the much-repeated official justification for the *Playboy* shoot that Gessat, and her teammates disrobed in order to prove that they were "totally normal, regular girls ("Mädel") who chose to play soccer but also love to shop and place a special value on their appearance," Frach points to the sad fact that millions of German male soccer fans will never know Gessat, the excellent and promising soccer player and fine athlete, but only the naked pin-up girl in come-hither poses.

While the posing in *Playboy* was without a doubt the most egregious example of the Women World Cup's sexualization in Germany, there were many other instances of featuring the players' beauty and sexuality though with clothes, often featuring them. Thus, for example, six members of the national team's senior squad, definitely more prominent football players and bigger stars than the five junior team members posing for *Playboy*, appeared in suggestive poses in many commercials for the shampoo company "Schwarzkopf" whose logo in English is "Professional HairCare for you" under such headlines as "our beauty-eleven storms straight to the final" or "soccer professionals can be this beautiful". And the German national team's Fatmire "Lira" Bajramaj was much more famous for being the country's "glamour girl" football player who, according to her widely-known views, never runs onto the field without lip gloss as well as mascara, and

---

[61] Henrik Frach, „Fußballspielerin oder Sexobjekt? Weiblichkeit und Sexualisierung im Frauenfußball" (unpublished research paper, University of Lüneburg, Lüneburg, Germany, summer 2011)

is eager to marry early, have two or three kids and open a cosmetics salon, than being the team's only player of Muslim and Albanian descent having been born in Kosovo and emigrating to Germany as a young girl.[62]

In addition to these depictions of the women players, little girls could also admire and play with a Barbie doll version of a member of the German women's team. The Barbie, released in time for 2011's World Cup, wore official German-soccer-federation-licensed miniature football gear identical to that of the real players over her certainly Barbie-like figure (i.e. busty and blonde). Just as all Barbies, this one also had visible makeup on her face, gloss on her lips, mascara on her eye lids, and embodied the hegemonic culture's picture-perfect femininity, even in her soccer cleats. The words "I can be…" appear both in English and in German (ich wäre gern,,,), followed by "Fußballspielerin" only in German (the feminine version of "soccer player"), clearly encouraging girls to engage in Barbie's sport, while simultaneously reinforcing all that Barbie's figure and appearance have come, after all these decades, to reinforce and represent symbolically though, it needs to be added, with recently launched laudable attempts by Mattel, Inc. to counter this conventionally feminine and often sexualized image.

---

[62] See, for example, "Die will nicht nur spielen!" in *Freundin*, 14/2011

The sexualization of the World Cup and female soccer players reached well beyond the established media. Thus, an innocuous visit by Janna Bray (a doctoral student in the Department of Political Science at the University of Michigan at the time, engaged in research in Berlin totally unrelated to the World Cup or any sports) to the town hall of Treptow-Köpernick, one of the German capital's important eastern districts, revealed five artful photo collages produced by students at the Merian School gracing this public building's entrance area. The first one, featuring the logo "Fußball ist…SEXY" (football is SEXY in large letters), depicted an attractive woman dressed in a soccer uniform, sitting on a soccer ball and sucking her fingers suggestively. The next image, with the text, "Auf die Party! Fertig! Los! Sie ist bereit, bist du es auch?" (Onward to the party! Ready! Go! She is ready, are you?), featured a mini-skirted woman's legs as they shed Nike soccer boots for stilettos. The third montage featured the text "Keine Angst Männer, es ist nur Fußball" (Don't worry, men, it is only soccer) and depicted a woman holding a gift-wrapped soccer ball across her belly clearly emulating pregnancy. The fourth item had a young woman kiss a glass case which held a frog and a soccer ball adorned with a crown. The caption read, "Ein Märchen wird wahr" (a fairy tale turns true). And lastly, accompanying the text "…und wir haben doch Ahnung von Technik, überzeugt euch selbst" (and we do know technique, find out for yourselves), we see a woman's long, bare legs clad in red stilettos kicking a soccer ball in the air with her left heel.[63]

This tone and content reached beyond Germany. In neighboring Austria where women's soccer plays even a lesser role than in most Central and West European countries and whose team did not even qualify for the World Cup tournament in Germany in 2011, *Sport Magazin,* Austria's most comprehensive and popular sports publication ran a huge spread on one of the country's players, a certain Mariella Rappold, the "ÖFB-Beauty" [ÖFB stands for Österreichischer Fußball-Bund, the Austrian Soccer Federation] whose absence in the tournament would, according to the publication, severely diminish the beauty quotient of the players in Germany and thus mar the competition's overall attractiveness and desirability a la "look what the fans in Germany will miss" decidedly referring to Rappold's attractive appearance and not her prowess as a soccer player.[64] Here, too, the sexualized double entendres appeared in virtually every paragraph of the article. And though Rappold did not pose nude for the camera, some of the published pictures – killer stilettos, miniskirts and all – clearly accentuated her looks rather than her skills as an athlete and soccer player. And one should never forget the context wherein this occurred: A continued marginalization of women's soccer in Germany and Austria. At least the former celebrated a World Cup in which solely the

---

[63] We are grateful to Janna Bray for having taken photographs of these five items during her visit to the Rathaus Treptow-Köpenick in Berlin on July 6, 2011, and for sharing them with us.

[64] "Mara-Donna Fußball" in *Sport Magazin*, July 2011, pp. 46 – 53.

power of nationalism weighed in and created a buzz for the women's game for a four-week period. But as Julia Zeeh's fine master's thesis at the University of Vienna, clearly shows, women's soccer in Austria continued to lead a woefully marginal existence as measured by every imaginable dimension. [65]

It was in 1982 that the German national team in women's football was founded. By 1989 the team captured its first European championship; additional titles followed in 1991, 1995, 1997, 2001, 2005, 2009 and 2013. Overall the German team has won eight EURO championships since the tournament's inception in 1984. This abundance of championships demonstrates decidedly that the German women footballers have become Europe's best, even surpassing their perennial Scandinavian rivals hailing from Norway and Sweden. This European excellence was soon to follow on the global stage. Attaining fourth place at the first official FIFA-sponsored and organized women's football world championship in China in 1991, the German team reached second place at the second World Cup tournament in Sweden in 1995 and then became world champion in the fourth tournament in the United States in 2003. The German national team defended its title in a most impressive manner at the fifth championship in China in the fall of 2007 in which it won the championship undefeated and unscored upon. Furthermore, the team won bronze at the Olympics in 2000, 2004, and

---

[65] Julia Zeeh, "Fankultur im Frauenfußball" Zugangsformen und Motivationen des Publikums beim SV Neulengbach" (unpublished Master's thesis, Department of Sociology, University of Vienna, 2012).

2008. After missing the qualification for the Olympics in 2012, the team finally won gold in 2016. In a matter of barely two decades, the German women had become a perennial powerhouse in the world of women's football surpassed only by the Americans in terms of ownership of prestigious tournament titles, trophies and medals.

But just like in England, excellence on the field has not translated into popularity of the women's game on the club level in Germany. Attendance in the 2013/14 averaged a meager 1,185 spectators per game.[66] The number decreased over the following years to an average of 846 in 2017/18.[67] VfL Wolfsburg was on top with an average of 1,689 with 1.FC Köln attracting an average of only 324 spectators per game. Although the numbers increase substantially when it comes to cup finals, or World Cup games (the average attendance during the World Cup 2011 in Germany was 26,428[68]), women's football became on the one hand immensely successful but has remained at the same time quite unpopular. The number of women *playing* football in Germany exceeds the number of people *watching* women's football by far.[69]

Only during World Cup victories does the German women's team overcome the obscurity and marginalization that have become normal

---

[66] "Frauen Bundesliga 2013/2014 » Zuschauer » Heimspiele", https://www.weltfussball.de/zuschauer/frauen-bundesliga-2013-2014/1/.
[67] "Frauen Bundesliga 2017/2018 » Zuschauer » Heimspiele", https://www.weltfussball.de/zuschauer/frauen-bundesliga-2017-2018/1/.
[68] "Durchschnittliche Zuschauerzahlen der FIFA Frauen-Weltmeisterschaften von 1991 bis 2015", https://de.statista.com/statistik/daten/studie/184621/umfrage/durchschnittliche-zuschauerzahl-der-frauen-fussball-wm-seit-1991, 2019.
[69] The number of women watching men's football should not be underestimated. Although women are confronted with sexism, they claim their place in that massively male space with increasing confidence.

fare during the long years and seasons between such rare international tournaments. Then, hundreds of thousands welcome the team at a parade on Frankfurt's "Römer", one of the city's best-known public squares. The throngs appear purely for nationalistic reasons, i.e. to celebrate a German victory on the world's stage rather than women's football. Most celebrants could not name more than two or three of the team's players, essentially confirming the German public's "olympianized" relation to this sport. Just like in the United States, too, as well as in many countries, the popularity of women's football in Germany remains inextricably tied to supporting solely a team that represents the nation. Football on the club level remains marginal on the women's side with no change in site. The women's game in Germany will not escape the giant shadow of the men's for decades to come, if ever.

The Scandinavian Countries: Denmark, Sweden, Norway

In a way, it is not at all surprising that the Scandinavian countries have assumed a leading role in the global development of women's football that is hugely out of proportion both with the percentage of these countries' population in the world and with their relatively modest presence and unspectacular results in the history of the men's game. But I argue that precisely because of the Scandinavian men's comparatively meager successes on all stages of global football (Denmark won the European national championship – the EURO - in a huge upset in 1992; and Sweden was the runner up to champion Brazil in the World Cup of 1958 hosted by Sweden and attained the bronze medal as the third-place finisher in the World Cup 1994 held in the United States; with IFK Goteborg being the only Scandinavian team ever to win one of Europe's coveted trophies – the UEFA Cup in 1982 and 1987 -- on the club level) and the early strides that women attained in many walks of life in these countries imbued with an unparalleled egalitarian ethic hailing from the institutional strength of social democracy in these countries; women's football in Denmark, Sweden and Norway was accorded a cultural space and an early legitimacy that few other countries offered anywhere in the world. Appropriately, in all three of these countries, women soccer players not only outnumbered their male counterparts in terms of the proportional entry/output of new players into organized soccer in 2004, but their proportional gains were only exceeded by – tellingly – the proportional presence of new women soccer players in the United States.

National Entry/Output of Female Football/Soccer Players in 2004[70]

	Total	Male	Female
The World a baseline)	1.00	1.00	1.00 (as
Europe	2.46	2.71	1.13
England	3.28	3.74	0.58
Germany	3.77	3.74	4.98
Norway			11.21
Denmark		3.31	6.64
Sweden		2.91	6.55
The United States	3.09	2.12	12.31
Canada		1.60	7.68
Brazil	2.03	2.28	0.11
Asia	0.46	0.50	0.03
China	0.28	0.30	0.03
Japan	1.30	1.47	0.08
South Korea	0.55	0.60	0.06

[70] Rosa Diketmüller, "Frauenfußball – Ein Paradigmenwechsel?" in
Eva Kreisky and Georg Spitaler (eds.) *Arena der Männlichkeit: Über das Verhätnis von Fußball und Geschlecht* (Frankfurt: Campus Verlag, 2006), p. 355.

I find this table useful for showing – albeit only for one year – the proportional presence of new female soccer players compared to their male counterparts in certain key countries. The table also provides some interesting inter-country comparisons. Thus, there is no doubt that the United States – not surprisingly – is the leader of the pack in terms of the disproportional entry/output of women players into organized soccer closely followed by Norway as the only other country boasting a double-digit index in the women's column.

Of the three Scandinavian countries here briefly presented, Denmark was arguably the earliest trailblazer in the world of women's football beyond the immediate confines of the country. Almost as a lark and most certainly as an advertising gimmick, the well-known Italian beverage company Martini & Rossi organized a women's football tournament in 1970 in Italy which it called the first women's world cup. Lacking any kind of official seal by any of the relevant institutions of football – be it the Italian, European or global football federations – and held completely outside of their purview, approval and jurisdiction, one could best characterize this event as a privately-organized international tournament of a few women's teams representing their countries.[71] In front of 50,000 spectators in Turin, Denmark defeated host Italy in the final by the score of 2 – 0.[72]

---

[71] Beate Fechtig, *Frauen und Fußball,* p. 31.

[72] Anne Brus and Else Trangbaek, "Asserting the Right to Play – Women's Football in Denmark" in Fan Hong and J.A. Mangan, (eds.) *Soccer, Women, Sexual Liberation: Kicking Off A New Era,* p. 104. It is interesting to note that Beate Fechtig in her important book *Frauen und Fußball* mentions the spectatorship for this game at 35,000. Whatever the correct number might be, it represents a respectable tally.

The team that won this tournament for Denmark was BK Femina, one of the best-known teams of women's Association football history and certainly one of the game's most prominent representatives of the pre-1970s era, almost comparable perhaps to England's Dick, Kerr Ladies. The team was founded in 1959 by a well-known Danish women's magazine called "Femina." One of Femina's male journalists, in his research on women's sports in Denmark, encountered a few women whom he encouraged to take up playing football after they had informed him that they would much rather play this game instead of team handball. The club, called Boldklubben Femina, became somewhat of a controversial sensation in Denmark. Spawning other clubs all over the country, there emerged the Danish Women's Football Union in the early 1960s which – until the admission of women's football into the official Danish Football Federation, DBU in 1972 – organized teams playing each other in this semi-official, semi-tolerated and often-ridiculed world of women's football. Of course, there were many obstacles. By 1962, the magazine "Femina" severed all relations with and financial support for BK Femina, the football club. One year later, when a few women's teams wanted to hold a tournament under the auspices of the Copenhagen Ball Games Association, their request was summarily denied by the official Danish federation with no explanations offered.

BK Femina dominated the women's game in Denmark by winning pretty much any and all titles and tournaments – and most of the games – that occurred with some, though far from established, regularity. BK Femina's first trip outside of Denmark was to Czechoslovakia where the Danish women played the women's side of the well-heeled Czech football and sport club Slavia Praha. The sole Danish journalist that covered this event wrote about "hard tackling and light make-up," and the photographs accompanying the article depicted one of the BK Femina players in her football jersey followed by another picture in which she appeared in a somewhat suggestive pose by the side of a swimming pool wearing a bikini.[73] BK Femina also played a central role in the establishment of the Federation of Independent European Female Football (FIEFF), a privately financed football association that organized the first – of course completely unofficial – European championship in women's football in Italy in 1969. BK Femina represented Denmark and lost to Italy in the final, a defeat that it would avenge exactly one year later in the aforementioned first world championship in the women's game. In September 1971, the first genuinely national Danish team, still very much centered on BK Femina players but comprising others as well, traveled to yet another world championship tournament, this time to Mexico, where it defeated the host nation for the title by a score of 3 – 0. All Danish goals were the

---

[73] Ibid., pp. 101 - 103

product of Susanne Augustesen, a 15-year old football wunderkind. This game was held in the presence of 100,000 spectators in Mexico City's famed Estadio Azteca, site of the men's World Cup final of 1970 between Brazil and Italy with the former winning the title for the third time and thus being bestowed the Jules Rimet Cup for keeps. Because the Danish Football Association – as well as FIFA – did not recognize the women's final between Denmark and Mexico as an official football event, this impressive attendance figure never entered football's official record books with the final match of the Olympic Games in 1996 attended by 76,489 spectators in Athens, Georgia, and its equivalent at the World Cup in the Rose Bowl in Pasadena, California with 90,185 people in attendance in 1999 still regarded as the two leading events having drawn the largest crowds anywhere in the world for any women's sport – or any event, for that matter, featuring women as its sole protagonists.[74]

Perhaps following these victories on an international (albeit still unofficial) stage, though much more likely due to the increasingly changing discourse towards women and gender in the liberal democracies of advanced capitalism at this time, the Danish Football Federation DBU finally accepted women into its fold in 1972. Interestingly, this incorporation not only led to an upgrading in the status and official presence of the women's game in Denmark, but it also

---

[74] The attendance figure of 100,000 for the game between the Danish and Mexican women's football teams in 1971 hails from Brus and Trangbaek.

commenced a gradual decline of the Danish women's prominence, perhaps even pre-eminence, in the world of women's football. For nothing was more sacrosanct to the Danish Football Federation than the unblemished amateurism of all its members and participants that – as of 1972 – also included all Danish female players and their teams. Gone were the days of sponsorships by women's magazines and Italian beverage companies. That was strictly verboten for any and all amateurs.

The Danish women's national team triumphed one last time at the still unofficial European championship in 1979 beating host Italy and reversing the outcome from exactly one decade earlier when Italy bested Denmark in the first such Europe-wide tournament also hosted in Italy. The victory in 1979 would be the Danish team's last triumph on the international stage. Other than in the tournament in 2017 when Denmark succumbed in the final match to the victorious Netherlands, the Danish women would never again reach the finals of any major football competition. Paradoxically, precisely by the time of the 1980s when the women's game would finally acquire its full institutional legitimacy and its official imprimatur by all relevant bodies that rule over the world of Association football, the Danish women footballers became mediocre and had to observe how their German and Scandinavian sisters in Sweden and Norway surpassed them as global players in the women's game.

The Swedish story follows the already well-known pattern. There were teams in Sweden in the 1910s and early 1920s, but the FA's banning of the women's game in England in 1921 was a welcome pretext for the Swedish male-dominated football establishment to do the same. In the 1950s and early 1960s there were women's games played occasionally, but these were much closer to publicity stunts than to genuine and sustained athletic activities.[75] Different from other European countries but distantly similar to the United States, Swedish universities came to play a pioneering role in the nascent days of the establishment of modern women's football in Sweden which – tellingly, just like everywhere else – commenced in the late 1960s and early 1970s. A football tournament occurred at Stockholm University in 1965, and similar competitions followed at universities in Gothenburg and Lund in 1967/68.[76] Even though the top office of the Swedish Football Association (SFF) did not fully and officially incorporate women's football into its purview until 1972, two of its regional associations established women's football leagues between 1969 and 1971. Interestingly (and tellingly), the women's league, started by the newspaper *Arbetet* in 1969 in the southern province of Skane (quite close to Denmark), was inspired by Danish women's football.

However, in marked contrast to most other European countries, Swedish sports journalists – almost exclusively male at the time just like

---

[75] Jonny Hjelm and Eva Olofsson, "A Breakthrough: Women's Football in Sweden" in Fan Hong and J.A. Mangan (eds.) , *Soccer, Women, Sexual Liberation: Kicking Off A New Era*, pp. 184, 185.
[76] Ibid.

everywhere else -- curtailed their disdain for women invading the all-male domain of football and, to their credit, described often in positive and understanding tones "how women struggled against traditional attitudes regarding appropriate jobs and activities for women...This does *not* mean that women's football was treated in the same manner as men's football – sexist comments such as 'football amazons' and 'Valkyres' were used when talking about women footballers...nor does it mean that the majority of sports journalists exhibited particularly positive attitudes towards women's football. However, strikingly many of those who wrote about women's football at that time, and who became 'women's football experts' for their newspapers, held a positive fundamental tone and willingly reported on the criticism of the pioneers within women's football aimed at SSF or at other local opposition to women's football."[77]

By 1973, Sweden fielded its very first official female national team in football. In its inaugural game, it played to a 0 – 0 draw against the team from Finland. In the above-mentioned very first – though still unofficial – European Championship in 1978 in Italy in which the Danish women triumphed, the Swedes attained third place. By the end of the 1980s, there were between 37,000 and 40,000 registered female footballers in Sweden. This level has essentially held steady since then. In the course of the 1980s and 1990s, the Swedish women have without

---

[77] Ibid, emphasis in the original.

a doubt attained a position of international excellence in women's football, only exceeded by their Norwegian neighbors, the Germans, and the Americans. Sweden organized the second official FIFA-sanctioned World Cup in 1995 in which the Norwegians won their first title. At the European Championship of 2001, the Swedish team attained second place. Some of Sweden's female players became among the most respected footballers in the game. Thus, Pia Sundhage, perhaps the country's best female player of all times, followed her playing days by being a successful head coach in the Women's United Soccer Association (WUSA) in America, which attracted the world's best of the best during its existence. Moreover, Sundhage was named in the fall of 2007 to become the sixth head coach of the United States women's national team, the first foreigner bestowed with such an honor. Barely one year into her tenure, Sundhage led Team USA to its third Olympic gold medal at the Beijing games in August of 2008 a feat she then repeated four years later at the Olympic Games in London in the summer of 2012. She also led the US women to second place behind Japan at the World Cup in Germany in 2011. As of December 1, 2012, Sundhage returned to her native Sweden to coach her country's women's national team in football which, irony of ironies, eliminated the United States in the quarterfinals of the 2016 Olympics in Rio de Janeiro making the Americans depart empty-handed for the first time ever from a World Cup or an Olympics, the two major tournaments in global women's football since 1991 and 1996 respectively.

Gauged by the accumulation of medals at the officially sanctioned seven World Cup and six Olympic tournaments in women's football since 1991, the Norwegian women with their five, (including gold in the World Cup of 1995 and the Olympics of 2000) only trail the Americans and the Germans. This is not surprising since – as evident in the afore-listed Table – the proliferation of the women's game in Norway, in terms of the entrance to playing football by women in relation to men, weighs in a close second to that in the United States. The gaps have been reduced since 2004 but not quite eliminated. Both countries remain ahead of the competition.

In Norway, too, the pre-1970s world of football was scattered, sporadic and essentially unknown to most Norwegians. Indeed, the very first meaningful and generally recognized women's game was not played until 1970 when Malfrid Kuvas, representing the sport club BUL, organized a match. Not surprisingly, she has come to be called the "mother of football" in Norway.[78] Like everywhere else, in the decade of the 1970s and 1980s, the women's game developed on all levels in Norway. Indeed, Karin Fasting, one of Norway's leading experts on Norwegian women's sports and an eminent university professor, linked the game's growth and successful establishment to "the second wave of

---

[78] Karin Fasting, "Small Country - Big Results: Women's Football in Norway" in Fan Hong and J.A. Mangan (eds.) , *Soccer, Women, Sexual Liberation: Kicking Off A New Era*, p. 150.

feminism" which commenced at the time and which featured a society-wide debate about women's rights in all aspects of public and private life that extended way beyond playing fields and athletic competitions.[79] Norway merely spearheaded a trend that happened at the time in virtually all countries of advanced industrial capitalism with a liberal democratic order.

One specific act of inclusion, however, might have rendered Norway unique among its European counterparts, even compared to the country's Scandinavian neighbors of Sweden and Denmark. Once the Norwegian Football Association (NFA) fully accepted the women's game in 1975 (actually a few years later than the other federations discussed in this chapter), the integration of women into the world of Association football commenced full throttle and with genuine enthusiasm exhibiting none of the foot dragging and reluctance that remained the case in so many of the still-predominantly male establishments in the other countries. The NFA established a Women's Committee in 1976 which – commencing in 1980 – placed much emphasis on the education and promotion of female managers, coaches, referees and officials in addition – of course – to the development of female players at every level of the game. The Women's Committee and its members "systematically worked to recruit girls and women to leadership, coaching and referee positions."[80] By 1999, Karen Espelund

[79] Ibid., p. 151.
[80] Ibid., p. 155.

had become the first female secretary general of the Norwegian Football Association and thus leader of all of Norwegian football, male and female. This was arguably the most powerful post in all of Norwegian sport. Espelund held among the most distinguished leadership positions among all Association football federations anywhere in the world, including the United States. Espelund became a member of the UEFA Women's Football Committee in 1990. Between 2012 and 2016, Espelund served on UEFA's executive committee, European football's most decisive leadership body.

In addition to the traditions of Scandinavian egalitarianism and the power of the second wave of feminism which clearly represent the prime reason for the successful proliferation of women's football in Norway, I would like to suggest another tradition which, yet again, makes Norway quite similar to the United States in the world of the women's association game: the relative cultural weakness and the low level of success of the men's game. Thus, it is surely not by chance that China, the United States, Japan, the two Koreas, Australia, Canada and Norway (countries in which the men's game has historically been at best mediocre and rarely, if ever, blessed with international accolades) have furnished national teams on the women's side that consistently rank among the top seven or eight in the world. Women succeeded *precisely* in countries where Association football was culturally not completely occupied by men, and thus did not fully constitute what I have termed 'hegemonic sports culture'. Put differently, the men's game did not dominate in the aforementioned countries – all major powers in the women's game at least periodically if not perennially since its rise to prominence -- at anywhere close to the level it has in the countries where the men's game has constituted the absolute core of hegemonic sports culture (the four British football nations; virtually all countries in continental Europe and in Latin America with the exception of a few Caribbean nations) , thus giving the women's game ample "space" to develop and flourish.

Women's EURO and UEFA Women's Champions League

Finally, to demonstrate the quantum leap in the development of women's football in Europe over the past three decades, a brief mention needs to be made of the two Europe-wide competitions that have been so central to the men's game: the UEFA Women's EURO, the quadrennial tournament of national teams; and the UEFA Women's Champions League, the annual club competition of the best club teams on the continent. Pertaining to the former, there were two preceding stages that are worthy of mention: The first, already listed above, involved the unofficial European tournaments held in Italy in 1969 and 1979 won by Italy and Denmark respectively. The second stage, commenced in 1982 with UEFA's full acceptance of women's football, witnessed a few tournaments held in slightly irregular intervals of three and two years respectively. The first such official tournament held under the aegis of UEFA occurred in 1984 with Sweden's emerging as the winner and England's as the runner up. In 1987, host Norway beat neighboring Sweden for the title; and in 1989 it was host West Germany that defeated Norway to capture its first of eight titles. The tournament was held in 1991, 1993 and 1995 with newly united Germany winning in 1991 and 1995 and Norway prevailing in 1993. As of 1997, the third stage commenced with the tournament mutating into a regularized quadrennial event completely equal to the men's, with Germany winning each championship excepting the last one in 2017 when host Holland defeated Denmark for its first title.

As to the most important Europe-wide club competition – the UEFA Women's Champions League – the first round commenced in the 2001-2002 season under the name UEFA Women's Cup only to be renamed Champions League in the 2009-2010 season thus creating full parity in nomenclature with the men's competition. In addition to the name change, two important reforms occurred in that season: the top eight women's national leagues commenced to place their top two teams into the competition and not just the league champions; the final became one game played on neutral ground instead of the previous home-and-home two-game contest. Lyon has thus far been the most successful team with five titles followed by Frankfurt with four.

Conclusion

To conclude this presentation of European women's football: The pattern is virtually identical in every country. The game proceeded from a world of semi-concealed and sporadic occurrences where it was little more than a marginalized curiosity, if not a freak show, to a massive opening in the 1970s and an eventual fully legitimized institutionalization throughout the 1980s and 1990s which has rendered the game at least formally equal to that of the men's. After all, the women's game has been played on the very same field as the men's (though still often on different surfaces with the women having to put up with the dangers, discomfort, health hazard and ignominy of playing on artificial turf while the men always play on grass) with the very same rules, the same number of players, during the same number of minutes, under the same organizational jurisdictions, in the same formats, from club championships and cup competitions to international tournaments on a continent-wide and global level. To arrive at this formal equality with the men's game, women footballers in Europe had to surmount a formidable hurdle in that they were compelled to enter a sacrosanct male world and contest the men in their most intimately guarded space. To do this, the women had to "gender bend," thus not only challenge the men in their encrusted domain but also counter hitherto accepted gender roles for women. Thus, it will not come as a surprise to the reader that in every single one of these European cases, women footballers are often associated by men and the male-dominated hegemonic discourse with lesbianism. After all, the perception goes that lesbians, who are stereotypically viewed as more masculine than heterosexual women, are the only ones who can really get so passionately engaged in the macho world of football. There can be no question that to many European men women footballers continue to constitute something profoundly threatening, in addition to being risibly inferior in the quality of their athleticism and their product on the field. Indeed, for some men in Europe there is something downright blasphemous about women playing this game. They simply do not belong in any of its facets. The road for women's soccer in America faced equally massive hurdles, though of a very different kind. It is to the game across the Atlantic to which I now turn.

CHAPTER THREE:

Women's Soccer in the United States: Trailblazer for women's sports, women's rights, and a more inclusive, thus democratic country

Introduction

The story of women's soccer in the United States features several nuances and developments that remain particular to the sport in America and bespeak soccer's unique status in the sports culture of the United States. Thus, I am reasonably certain that, with over five million known female soccer participants, the United States was at the beginning of the 21st century near or at the very top of a list of countries with such athletes.[81] More recent data show the number to be closer to between nine and ten million registered female soccer players, according to the FIFA Women's Football Survey from 2014.[82] Indeed, during the first decade of the 21st century, one third of all registered female soccer players in the whole world resided in the United States of America.[83] FIFA's own data hailing from 2006 corroborate my argument that nowhere is the game of Association football as female as in the United States. Data from 2014 confirm this point showing that nearly fifty percent of female soccer players in the entire world registered with FIFA

---

[81] US Soccer Foundation, 'Soccer in the USA, 2002-2003', p. 5. The exact figure for 2008 was 8,862,000. This consists of all females who have played the game at least once during the previous year. The figure for American males was 10,390,000; the combined total for both genders is 19,042,000.

[82] FIFA, "Women's Football Survey 2014," p. 50. The total number of female players for USA and Canada was 15,877,400 with the average total of each country being 7,938,700 female soccer players.

[83] Rosa Diketmüller, "Frauenfußball – Ein Paradigmenwechsel?", p. 353.

come from the United States and Canada, with the former contributing more players than the latter. These two nations have the highest volume of female soccer players anywhere in the world, compared with the other member associations within FIFA. Total female players registered in FIFA were 30,145,700. The United States and Canada contributed 15,877,400.[84] In the Confederation of North, Central American and Caribbean Association Football (CONCACAF), FIFA's regional organization to which the United States belongs, of the 43,109,000 soccer players (both registered and unregistered) 10,038,000 (or 26 percent) were female. In UEFA, Europe's region, women hovered at just shy of 10 percent and in South America they barely reached 11 percent.[85] FIFA attempted a more recent big count for release in 2011 but this survey was never completed. While these CONCACAF data do not specifically single out the United States, I am reasonably certain that this disproportionately large number of female players does not hail from Mexico, Central America or the Caribbean in particular since other data from the same study do in fact offer helpful corroborating evidence pertaining to the United States. With its 1,670,000 registered female players, the United States Soccer Federation was the only federation in the world that had more than one million female members during the first decade of the 2000s and thus lead the runner up – Germany's Deutscher Fußball-Bund (DFB) with its 871,000 female members at the

[84] 2014 FIFA Women's Football Survey, p. 48.
[85] FIFA Big Count 2006: Statistical Summary Report by Gender/Category/Region

time – by almost double. This leadership position of the United States in the number of women soccer players also pertains to youth soccer. Here, the United States lead Germany in all categories, with the gap between girls — at 1,563,000 for the United States and 237,000 for Germany — being more than seven-fold in 2006.[86] More recent data show a continuation of this situation in 2015, with 94% of all registered female soccer players in the United States being youth players. This compares to only 31% in Germany.[87] Americans also comprise over 50% of all the world's registered female youth soccer players.[88]

Moreover, beyond the importance of these quantitative figures, it is the quality of this presence that renders the status of women's soccer in the United States so different in comparison to its position in other countries. In few countries has women's soccer been the cultural equivalent of – or even superior to -- the men's game. After all, Michelle Akers, Julie Foudy, Mia Hamm, Brandy Chastain, Joy Fawcett of the US women's national team's first generation and Megan Rapinoe, Carli Lloyd, Alex Morgan, Tobin Heath of its second with the legendary Abby Wambach and the timeless Kristine Lilly and Heather O'Reilly forming sort of a bridge between the two have been probably more widely known as soccer players (as opposed to media figures) than virtually all their male equivalents and contemporaries in the United States, be they of the

[86] Ibid.
[87] https://fivethirtyeight.com/features/why-is-the-u-s-so-good-at-womens-soccer/
[88] Ibid.

Alexi Lalas (1990s) or the Landon Donovan (2000s) generation though this may change with Christian Pulisic's rising in our current era. Prominent network news anchors would most assuredly not have mangled any of these female stars' names as one did with Landon Donovan's, to whom he referred as "Langdon Donovan" in an interview with David Beckham on the "Today Show" in July 2009. It goes without saying that any anchor, not just this one, would also not have committed a similar error in his mentioning any comparable star's name from the North American Big Four sports of baseball, football, basketball and hockey. Nor would any European news anchors mangle the names of their respective countries' top-level male football stars though they might very well have difficulty knowing the names of their women players. Neighboring Canada might in fact offer a parallel construct to the situation in the United States in that Christine Sinclair has enjoyed an arguably greater status of celebrity in that country than any of its male soccer players.

The exception of America's position in soccer in general and women's soccer in particular is best embodied by a fascinating project in which FIFA, on the occasion of its centenary in 2004, asked Pele, by common consensus (pace Diego Maradona) the greatest player the game has ever known (at least until Lionel Messi and Cristiano Ronaldo), to compose a list of the 100 players whom he deemed the finest footballers still alive on the planet. Pele could not confine himself to 100 and delivered a list of 125 players. His home country of Brazil led the way with 15 names, followed by Italy and France with 14 each, the Netherlands next at 13, Argentina and Germany with 10 each and England with seven. The only American soccer players that made Pele's list were Michelle Akers and Mia Hamm, who were also, of course, the only women among the 125 chosen by the legend. It goes without saying that no American male soccer player made Pele's list. Bespeaking the football world's dismissive views of American and women's soccer, many a football commentator in Latin America and Europe was outraged that the Brazilian great had dared "waste" two of his precious spots for American players – and women to boot. In defending his choice of including two women (and Americans no less) on his list, Pele said: "I confused the people I was working with, but I believe that female football is very important today."[89]

Moreover, in no other country would it be possible – or even conceivable -- for women players to serve as the expert (i.e., 'color') commentators on national television, explaining the intricacies of the men's game to a largely male viewing public. But this has occurred with regularity in the United States over the last two decades during all men's World Cup tournaments as well as other important national and international soccer games. Can anybody imagine that in *any* European or Latin American country the expert commentator – the Gary Lineker

[89] "Pele names top 125", http://foxsports.news.com.au/print/0,8668,8874487-23215,00.html , March 5, 2004.

in England, the Günter Netzer in Germany – would be a woman? In other words, can anybody in Europe picture a situation in which the absolute final and most respected authority, interpreting the nuances of the game and the intricacies of events on and off the field to millions of male viewers, might be a woman? Unthinkable – but not in the United States, at least in the world of soccer. In this game, women have true authority in America. And remember, I do not mean play-by-play commentators or sideline reporters the former of which they have come to represent here and there; the latter of which they have come to dominate. Rather, I am concentrating here on the color commentator, the expert in the studio, the voice that lends gravitas to the broadcast by informing the audience of the intricacies of the game by virtue of having experienced it first hand as a star player. Cases in point: Julie Foudy and Joy Fawcett for ESPN or Aly Wagner for Fox simply do not have their analogous equivalents in countries in which Association football has hegemonic culture. To be sure, a few women have entered the broadcast booth for football matches in England and in Germany over the past ten years. But they have always been journalists who report on players or teams or even plays in matches, but they have not been former players who, by dint of their experience on the pitch, enhance the broadcast's legitimacy and authority to a predominantly male audience. Former American women soccer players have become legitimate experts with authoritative voices vis-a-vis male soccer audiences that their European counterparts simply have not.[90]

Thus, it is never the inherent gestalt of the sport itself that defines its gendered identity. Rather, it is the respective sport's position in the history and structure of a country's respective sports space and its hegemonic sports culture: simply put, if the sport – regardless of its specific form and content -- has been central to the history and structure of these spaces, it will be heavily male and virtually exclusive of, perhaps even hostile to, women. If the sport has not been central to these spaces, it will be more welcoming to women.

This chapter presents the contours of the reasons, origins, and present manifestations of a specific American sports exception: the prominence of women's soccer in the United States where the game had historically been quite marginal in terms of its cultural presence. I offer a brief history of women's soccer in the United States before I concentrate on the game's various constituents and their development in recent years. Specifically, I present the game's recreational manifestations as well as its competitive dimensions, ranging from youth league, high school, and college soccer all the way to the professional game as embodied in the Women's United Soccer Association (WUSA), its successor, Women's Professional Soccer (WPS) and the current league

---

[90] There have been interesting recent developments regarding the featuring of women as color commentators in the broadcasting of baseball and basketball, two of the four essential cultural representatives of American hegemonic sports. Doris Burke (a Hall of Famer) in basketball and Jessica Mendoza in baseball have emerged as important trailblazers in this crucial role of interpretation and evaluation of two staples of male culture. Both, of course, have faced derision and irritation by male audiences.

since its inception in 2012, the National Women's Soccer League (NWSL). Of course, I will devote some space to a discussion of the American women's national team, a fascinating entity all its own. I will conclude this chapter with some thoughts regarding the future of women's soccer in the United States, especially pertaining to its inevitable interaction with the men's game, and how -- if at all -- it might possibly contribute toward making soccer and/or women's sports a significant part of America's sports culture. Specifically, I will entertain the question whether the excellence of women as sports producers could in fact change women's sports consumption and thus alter a country's sports culture. Put differently, will millions of women as a rule (not as an exception, as outliers, what I termed "sportistas") ever breathe, eat, sleep, hope, study, and revere sport the way men do?

Though women's sports in general, and women's soccer specifically, have followed a much different trajectory than that experienced by men's team sports some similarities in their respective evolutionary paths are apparent. The Big Four in the United States (and men's soccer in most other countries) all underwent a process of 'modernization' -- mostly during the crucial period of 1870 to 1930 -- on their way to becoming primary occupants of the cultural 'sports space' in these societies. Initially, games for children and youths became the venues of recreation for adults, but initially with participation and camaraderie as their sole purpose. Eventually, however, the ethos of casual games for exercise and fellowship ('playing for fun') gave way to organized competition with victory as its predominant, perhaps even sole, purpose, reason and aim.[91] In the United States, this transformation occurred in men's team sports at every level (including interscholastic and intercollegiate competition). This development coincided with the creation of formal organization and ongoing 'rationalization' of the sport, regardless as to whether a specific sport ever achieved a following much beyond the actual participants on the field (or court) of play.[92]

However, the history of women's team sports in general -- and soccer in particular -- diverges from this timeline, as participatory recreation almost always superseded the drive for competition over a long period, at least until the 1970s. This was the case particularly at those institutions which represent a key facet of American sports (and comprise yet another American exception[93]), as well as perhaps the most important foci for the development of women's sports and women's soccer in the United States: The athletic programs at the nation's colleges and universities which are completely unique to the United States and do not exist in such fashion in any other country in the world, including Britain and its Commonwealth. Indeed, for all intents and

[91] See Warren Goldstein, *Playing for Keeps: A History of Early Baseball* (Ithaca, NY: Cornell University Press, 1989); and Andrei S. Markovits and Steven L. Hellerman, *Offside: Soccer and American Exceptionalism* (Princeton: Princeton University Press, 2001), pp. 13-33.

[92] See Allen Guttmann, *From Ritual to Record: The Nature of Modern Sports* (New York: Columbia University Press, 1978), and Markovits and Hellerman, *Offside*, pp. 23-33.

[93] This small publication does not permit a lengthy discourse on the well-known concept of "American exceptionalism". Suffice it to say that I employ this term strictly in its empirical not its normative sense meaning that I intend it to denote an American "difference" not an American "superiority" of any kind. The "difference" pertains to an implicitly understood European (and often global) norm.

purposes, American colleges and universities have become one of the major venues of producing the world's best athletes in the most varied sport disciplines with women's soccer being among the most salient.[94] Remember how the protagonist in the wonderful movie "Bend it like Beckham" crowns her soccer dreams by winning a full scholarship to play for a university in California the non plus ultra in development of women's soccer at the time and still today.

Once a competitive team sport has achieved a sufficient level of 'rationalization,' it may attract some measure of spectatorship and following from modest numbers of enthusiasts. In the United States, sports like lacrosse and volleyball – played by both men and women at the college, semi-professional, and (more recently) professional levels – have progressed to this point and not much further (though each has its relatively small coterie of supporters at various geographic and institutional locales).

But with men's soccer throughout most of the world and the Big Four in the United States, taking the next step proved decisive: Charismatic entrepreneurs succeed in producing and marketing the sport, its games, and its participants while institutionalizing an organized structure for the sport accompanied by firmly attaching the identification of teams to geographic areas or – in the case of college athletics -- institutions. Hence, enter the era of professional players, managers,

[94] See Markovits and Hellerman, *Offside*, pp. 42-44.

coaches, owners— the protagonists of modern sport culture. I have argued in a number of my previous publications that for a sport to have successfully penetrated a nation's sports space this process need to have begun by the last decade of the 19th century and best be completed in large discernable contours, if not in minute details, by the 1920s.[95] However, in the case of women's soccer (and women's sports in general) in the United States, the modernization process did not really commence until the last three decades of the twentieth century, at which point the sport's evolution accelerated quite dramatically.

---

[95] See Markovits and Hellerman, *Offside*, Chapter 2. Here I am following the pathbreaking work of Seymour Martin Lipset and Stein Rokkan who argued that it was during this temporal window that the topography of party systems in most Western democracies became ensconced and encased.

The Rise of Recreational Soccer in America

Any analysis regarding the proliferation of women's soccer as either recreational activity or spectator sport requires highlighting two key milestones separated by a full generation in time. The first was the passage of Title IX of the 1972 Federal Education Amendments to the Civil Rights Act of 1964 (subsequently strengthened by Congressional legislation in 1988). The second came with the success of the 1999 Women's World Cup (held in the United States) in attracting significant numbers of attendees and -- more importantly -- television viewers, along with the concurrent success of Team USA on the field and in garnering a wide and popular following of fans among the general public, many with little or no previous interest in soccer and/or women's sports. The years between 1972 and today have come to witness the popular proliferation of soccer on college campuses, at high schools, and as a recreational activity for boys and girls throughout the United States. This occurred particularly emphatically among middle class and upper middle-class families in America's suburbs and exurbs, mostly through participation in organized youth leagues and scholastic athletic programs.

Much of the acceptance and popularity for recreational soccer (but not, significantly, soccer as a spectator sport, nor its attendant culture of consumption as found elsewhere in the world) coincided with and was perhaps even directly attributable to -- and arguably the most significant legacy of -- the ill-fated North American Soccer League (NASL) of 1967 to 1985. The NASL was a professional venture that featured some of the greatest players of the game (most notably and conspicuously the legendary Pele playing alongside the equally legendary Franz "Kaiser" Beckenbauer on a New York Cosmos team that beat some of the finest clubs in the world and, by dint of the multi-nationality of its players, became a harbinger and trailblazer of what top-level football clubs came to constitute barely twenty years later) and the closest thing to offering routine quality first division soccer Americans had seen up to that point. It was the NASL that provided a legitimacy for the sport among the American professional and commercial managerial classes who desired a game for their children that was allegedly non-confrontational, nonviolent, 'multicultural', often co-educational, noncompetitive, and apart from – as well as superior to -- what many of the upscale and educated viewed as the crass and crude milieu of the Big Four. The latter, of course, was precisely the very world represented by football in all of Europe and much of Latin America, but the game's decidedly proletarian image and milieu there was immaterial to its perception as well as reality in the United States. Suddenly, soccer in America allowed upper middle-class suburban children of cosmopolitan parents who only drank the finest French wines, traveled to Europe repeatedly, drove Volvos and Saabs, and considered most mainstream and traditional aspects of American life – including the Big Four sports –

crude and uncultured, to participate in a newly acquired politically correct team sport. This milieu constructed soccer totally antithetically to its existence in countries where it constituted hegemonic sports cultures. In America soccer at first developed into a non-competitive, collective, tolerant, inter-gendered, democratic, cosmopolitan, and non-teleological sport in which results did not matter only participation did. It became the clear American "anti-football" preferred by the country's bi-coastal upper-middle class Europhile milieu which viewed American football (and the other three of the Big Four) as brutal, macho, linear, teleological and totally result-oriented ("winning is not everything, it is the only thing" as coined by the legendary coach of the champion Green Bay Packers Vince Lombardi, an icon of American sports culture).

This proliferation of recreational soccer for children 'from above' placed the focus for play almost entirely in organized leagues under the auspices of national organizations such as the American Youth Soccer Organization (AYSO), United States Youth Soccer Association (USYSA), and the Soccer Association for Youth (SAY), as well as more recently formed groups that had the purpose of developing 'elite' soccer talent: the Super Y-League and US Club Soccer. This path represents an obvious divergence from the ways in which soccer took root in nations where it does indeed represent hegemonic sports culture: 'from below,' from the street as it were, as the unstructured pastime and feral passion of the masses, where kids (almost exclusively boys) play the game on their own in the alleys, playgrounds, and sandlots as each of the Big Three took root in the United States (think stick ball, pick-up games, street ball, and hoops in driveways) and hockey in Canada (the frozen pond down the street, the ice-covered backyard) thus comprising the Big Four team sports of North America's hegemonic sports culture.

By nearly every measure, soccer's recreational surge in the United States has been truly impressive, indeed meteoric: In 1980, the total combined registration for the three aforementioned youth soccer leagues (AYSO, USYSA and SAY) stood at 888,705; in 2006 it had increased to 3,907,000[96]. As of 2017, that total has passed 4,000,000 with over three million of those players being registered with USYSA.[97] A breakdown of these figures according to gender shows male registration at 2,344,000 and female registration at 1,563,000[98]. An estimation of AYSO registration of six- to eighteen-year-olds for 2001-2002 provides totals of approximately 348,000 registered girls and 317,000 boys.[99] As of 2014, 48% of USYSA players are between 10 and 14 years of age, for roughly 1,440,000 players. The second highest age percentage came in at 37% of players who were under 10 years of age.[100] According to data from the Soccer Industry Council of America (SICA) hailing from 2000, there were 17,734,000 soccer players in the United States, of whom

[96] Fifa report, Page 11.
[97] http://rapidsyouthsoccer.org/us-youth-soccer-player-statistics/
[98] Ibid.
[99] John Enriquez, Registration Manager for the American Youth Soccer Organization (AYSO), personal communication, 9 December 2002. These figures represent an estimate compiled from a total of AYSO team rosters reported for either 2001 or 2002.
[100] http://rapidsyouthsoccer.org/us-youth-soccer-player-statistics/

8,436,000 were female. The average age of all players was 15.3.[101] There are currently over 24 million soccer players in the United States. As of 2014, USYSA reported that the gender breakdown of its teams and leagues is nearly equal, with 52% of its players identifying as male and 48% of players identifying as female. The median age of all USYSA's players, both male and female, was 11.5 years.[102] According to FIFA data from 2014, 54% of the United States' and Canada's registered female soccer players were under 17 years of age amounting to 1,217,700 players.[103] During the last two decades of the twentieth century, soccer became the second favorite participatory team sport in the United States, trailing only basketball and surpassing baseball by a wide margin. And though the combined totals for baseball and its 'sibling' softball remain ahead of soccer when participants of all ages are considered, this is not the case regarding both the under-18 and under-12 age groups, where soccer emerges slightly ahead.[104]

In terms of overall soccer participation, the increase in the number of female players has continued, while the overall number of male players in the United States has declined. According to the Sporting Goods Manufacturers Association, a trade group, there were 9.0 male

---

[101] As cited in Anson Dorrance, *The Vision of a Champion: Advise and Inspiration from the World's Most Successful Women's Soccer Coach* (Ann Arbor, Michigan: Huron River Press, 2002), p. 17.
[102] http://rapidsyouthsoccer.org/us-youth-soccer-player-statistics/
[103] 2014 FIFA Women's Football Survey, p. 49.
[104] US Soccer Foundation, 'Soccer in the USA, 2002-2003', p. 15. Total participants for basketball: 38,663,000; soccer: 19,042; softball: 17,679; baseball: 11,405. Soccer participants in the under-18 age group stands at 14,972,000, compared to 6,445,000 for softball and 8,119 for baseball (combined: 14,564000). The number for soccer participants under twelve years of age is 8,775,000, compared to 2,742,000 for softball and 4,731,000 for baseball (combined: 7,473,000).

participants and 5.4 females per one hundred people in 1987. In 2001 there were 8.6 male participants and 6.7 female participants per one hundred people (a decline of 4.4 percent and an increase of 24.1 percent, respectively). A study released in 2006 indicates that the respective numbers were 7.1% for males and 3.7% for females[105]. The definition of "participant" included all those who had played some soccer at least once during the previous year. Among five to twelve-year-old children, there were 4.9 million boys (a rate of 28 percent) and 2.5 million girls (23.3 percent) who fit this description. In 2017, according to Sports & Fitness Industry Association (SFIA), there were over 11 million people who participated in outdoor soccer, and of those 11 million, over 6.6 million played at a casual level, meaning at least once in the past year.[106] SFIA reported that 64% of all participants were male and 36% female, making the total number of male participants around 4,265,000 and female circa 2,400,000.[107] From 2012-2017, SFIA reported a decrease of less than 1 percent in total casual participation meaning that the amount of people playing outdoor soccer at least once a year remained steady during these five years. There was however, a more than 3 percent decrease in core participation meaning among those who played outdoor soccer at least once every 2 weeks, or more than 26 times per year.[108] Most impressive was the increase of over 700 percent in the number of

---

[105] SGMA, 2006 Soccer Participation Report, Page 7
[106] https://medium.com/@sfia/soccer-participation-in-the-united-states-92f8393f6469
[107] Ibid.
[108] Ibid.

girls playing organized varsity and junior varsity soccer in high schools over a twenty-year period: from 41,119 players in 1980-81 to 292,086 players in 2000-01.[109] As of 2014, the number of girls playing high school soccer has increased to about 375,000, making it the third most popular sport for girls in high school, trailing only basketball and volleyball, but ahead of baseball and softball.[110]

The exponential rise in the number of American girls playing organized and competitive soccer in high schools and recreational leagues has provided a solid foundation for women's soccer at both the college and professional levels. This was well exemplified by the success of the American team at the inaugural Under-19 Women's World Championship in September 2002 in Edmonton, Alberta. The United States dominated in winning its first five matches (by scores of 5-1, 4-0, 6-0, 6-0, and 4-1, veritable landslides in the world of soccer) on the way to eventually defeating the host team Canada in the final, a 1-0 overtime thriller.[111] Perhaps the greatest indicator for the relatively high levels of esteem and status attained by youth and women's soccer in the United States was the appearance of the newly-crowned champion American women's U-19 team on the cover of (and in a full feature article inside) *Soccer America*, the sport's premier magazine in the United States. It is well-nigh impossible and unimaginable that a similar accomplishment by young women would ever garner such prominent

[109] US Soccer Foundation, 'Soccer in the USA, 2002-2003', p. 16.
[110] https://fivethirtyeight.com/features/why-is-the-u-s-so-good-at-womens-soccer/
[111] Scott French, 'Déjà vu', *Soccer America*, 57, 19 (23 Septemeber 2002), pp. 8-13.

exposure and coverage in the comparable publication of any European country (say, for example, "Kicker" and "Elf Freunde" in Germany; or "4-4-2" and "When Saturday Comes" in Britain to mention just a few prominent ones among many) where soccer — as played by men — has achieved the status of hegemonic sports culture.

The U-19 team became a U-20 team in 2006, and a U-19 team was not reinstated until 2015, but it no longer competes for world titles as that is the purview of the USA U-20 team. The last major accomplishment of the U-19 team was a third-place finish in the U-19 Women's World Cup in Thailand in 2004.[112] The U-20 team is one of the best in the world, but has struggled in World Cup appearances, finishing fourth in Russia in 2006 and losing the quarterfinals in Germany in 2010. The team had one of its best years in 2012, winning the CONCACAF championship by a combined margin of 18-1 goals in all its matches. The team only lost 2 matches during the entire regular season in which they compiled a 17-2-2 record.[113]

[112] https://www.ussoccer.com/us-under20-womens-national-team/about-the-team
[113] Ibid.

The College Game: Essential Ingredient of Women's Soccer Success in America[114]

The roots of women's soccer at American colleges go back much further than the inclusion of Title IX in federal legislation, though it could be said that the 'modern era' of the game commences with Title IX in 1972. The beginning of this modern era coincided perfectly with the very years (1970 – 1974) during which in all the European examples I mentioned above women's football was finally recognized officially by the male football establishment. Physical education for girls and young women in the United States started to gain some measure of acceptance at women's colleges and girls' prep schools towards the end of the nineteenth century, though competitive sports for females was still frowned upon in many places.[115] Women were playing soccer on the campuses of the Seven Sisters colleges in the Northeast as part of intramural programs and at the direction of physical education departments in the early 1900s. Let us not forget in this context the pioneering work of Senda Berenson at Smith College who, as a newly arrived instructor on campus, adapted basketball that had just been invented by Dr. James Naismith in nearby Springfield, Massachusetts, in

---

[114] Unless otherwise specified, the information for this section on women's collegiate soccer in the US is derived from Shawn Ladda, 'The Early Beginnings of Intercollegiate Women's Soccer in the United States', *The Physical Educator*, 57, 2 (Spring 2000), 106-112. Accessed through Lexis-Nexis search, Wilson Web: *http://vweb.hwwilsonweb.com/cgi-bin/webcl*; and Shawn Ladda, 'The History of Intercollegiate Women's Soccer in the United States', Doctoral Dissertation, Columbia University, 1995.

[115] Women were playing basketball at Vassar and Smith colleges in 1892, barely a year after Dr. James Naismith had invented the game. See Bill Gutman, *The History of NCAA Basketball* (New York: Crescent Books, 1992).

1891, to become an integral part of the physical education curriculum for Smith students as early as 1892. Berenson, a member of the Naismith Basketball Hall of Fame, produced a women's version of basketball that, with changes here and there, remained the game played by women until – once again – the early 1970s, that crucial watershed for so many aspects of public life in the advanced capitalist countries with liberal democratic regimes. A book entitled *Field Hockey and Soccer Rules for Women*, published by Frost and Cubberley in 1923, indicates acceptance of both sports into the physical education curriculum for girls at the elementary, middle, and high school levels, and for young women in college. Both sports originated in Europe and proliferated as recreation for females in the United States. Yet field hockey was by far the more popular and more socially valued. The United States Field Hockey Association was founded at Bryn Mawr College in 1922, while women's soccer would establish no such overarching organization until the 1980s. Hence, many proponents of girls' and women's soccer during the first half of the twentieth century viewed the sport as a 'forerunner for field hockey'. Though soccer was played by women on campus in earlier years, the oldest records denoting the game are from 1924 at Smith College, where the women's athletic program allowed and promoted the formation of regular teams and the playing of competitive matches at the "interhouse, interclass, and intramural" levels. Most women's athletics occurred as part of the "play days" featured as a component of an established physical education program. A large majority of women's athletic and/or physical education departments viewed intercollegiate competition as "elitist", instead preferring egalitarian participation for the sake of physical fitness and recreation for all over competitiveness (i.e., teams composed of only the best players) with winning as the goal. Heeding to this view of fostering "egalitarian" participation in lieu of "elitist" winning, most women's athletic programs banned intercollegiate competition in all team sports; Smith introduced such a ban starting in the 1940s. This exclusion was to last until 1971.

The first known intercollegiate competition involving women's soccer occurred in the 1950s among several Vermont colleges. It is unclear which of these teams were given the status of varsity (where today funding and administration of the sport and its team would originate in a school's athletic department) or were considered clubs (funded through student activities organizations). Regardless, the women playing soccer at Johnson State College, Castleton State College, and Lyndon State College (where the players did indeed receive a varsity 'letter', making Lyndon State the first school in the country to do so) represented an evolution from informal recreation for its own sake to competitive contests between two organized teams from separate institutions. Additionally, women's soccer teams from the Canadian universities of Bishops, McDonald, and McGill also participated in matches against the Vermont schools. The team hosting the match determined the rules, since specific aspects of the game were sometimes in dispute. After the game, the players from both squads usually met for a meal or snacks and beverages in the host school's dining room.[116]

By the late 1960s, the National Association for Girls and Women in Sport (NAGWS) -- the organization with the most control over women's athletics in the United States at the time -- had changed its philosophy to accept and promote competitive varsity programs for women. NAGWS would eventually evolve into the Association for Intercollegiate Athletics for Women [AIAW], which in turn became subsumed by the National Collegiate Athletic Association [NCAA] in 1982.[117] Thus, not until 1982 did most collegiate sports – male and female – become governed by this very powerful body, establishing numeric approximation and at least nominal status equality between male and female participation and representation in this very important world of American sports culture. Even institutionally, let alone in terms of social and cultural acceptance, female collegiate sport in America remained separate from the men until 1982.

---

[116] The post-game socializing with meals and/or beverages is somewhat reminiscent of the milieu for the earliest baseball games between organized clubs of middle class men in New York (c. 1845-1855) and the earliest games of what would evolve into American football between students from Harvard and organized clubs in the Boston area and, more importantly, students from Harvard and McGill University (c. late 1860s through the early 1870s). In the case of these nineteenth century contests, the post-game activities were often considered equal to or even more important than the game itself. See Markovits and Hellerman, *Offside*, pp. 55-57, 71-73.

[117] The National Collegiate Athletic Association (NCAA) is by far the most important organization lording over college athletics in the United States. Excepting junior and community colleges, there are two other institutions governing American college sports: The United States Collegiate Athletic Association (USCAA); and the National Association of Intercollegiate Athletics (NAIA).

As the ethos of women's sports changed to accept intercollegiate competition, the Seven Sister schools added soccer as a team sport, complete with competition among schools. However, it was Brown University in 1975 that gained the distinction of being first to bestow varsity representational status on a soccer team at the beginning of what might be considered the 'modern era' of women's sports. Additionally, schools such as Castleton (which granted official status to its team the same year as Brown), Cortland State College in New York, Cornell University, Colgate University, the University of Rochester, and State University of New York-Albany were fielding squads for intercollegiate matches at this time. By 1978, the New England Intercollegiate Women's Soccer Association could count at least thirteen teams with such varsity status representing universities in the northeast, as well as an additional sixteen schools fielding teams designated as "clubs" (and eleven schools with teams of unknown status). That same year saw the first Ivy League Tournament for women's soccer. By the end of the decade the sport was being played by squads with club and university status throughout the nation. The first intercollegiate national championship tournament for women's soccer, sponsored by the AIAW, was held in 1981. Anson Dorrance, legendary coach of the University of North Carolina's "dynasty" soccer team and arguably one of the great coaches in all North American sports (male and female), had nothing but praise for the AIAW and credited its open-mindedness towards soccer and its unfailing support for all women's varsity sports as the decisive agent in creating, fostering and legitimating women's athletic activities on America's college campuses.[118] The following year, the NCAA -- having expanded its domain to include women's collegiate athletics -- sponsored the first National Championship Tournament for Women's Soccer.

The proliferation of women's sports on campus further accelerated in 1988 with passage by the United States Congress of the Civil Rights Restoration Act that widened the interpretation and enforcement of Title IX, making compliance with gender equity regulations a priority for most college athletic programs. Women's soccer has been a special beneficiary of Title IX, as the sport can provide a college with the opportunity to include a sizeable number of female student-athletes on a team. And since the law demands that every college and university that receives federal funds demonstrate a clear commitment to award an equal number of athletic scholarships for women as for men, and since college football teams alone offer 85 scholarships to men, women's soccer teams have become convenient mechanisms for colleges to counterbalance the men's football teams with a minimum of 14 such spots.

The growth of women's soccer as an intercollegiate sport since the early 1980s has been truly phenomenal. In 1982, a total of 103 colleges

---

[118] Anson Dorrance, *The Vision of a Champion*, p. 4.

– representing 10.2 percent of NCAA member schools – fielded varsity teams for a total of 2,743 players. In 2001, there were varsity teams from 930 colleges (78.6 percent of NCAA member schools) for a total of 21,709 players[119]. It is somewhat noteworthy that there were nearly 180 fewer men's varsity soccer programs (752) than women's in 2001.[120] As of 2017, there are 206 NCAA Division I men's teams, and 333 Division I women's teams. Between all three NCAA divisions, there are over 1,000 women's soccer teams in the country today.[121]

Women's soccer started to outdraw men's soccer in attendance as well. Six men's teams from NCAA Division I schools averaged over 2,000 spectators in 2001, while no women's teams did so (though Texas and North Carolina both managed to average at least 1,900). Sixteen men's squads topped one thousand in average attendance that year, compared to twelve for women's teams.[122] In 2006, two women's teams, the University of Portland and Texas A&M University averaged over 3,000 spectators[123]. No men's soccer team averaged over 3,000 spectators, although nine men's teams drew over 2,000 spectators while only 3 women's teams managed to draw more than 2,000 spectators. The most recent highly attended women's soccer games occurred in 2014

[119] U.S. Census, http://www.census.gov/compendia/statab/tables/08s1220.pdf
[120] 'NCAA Sport-By-Sport Participation and Sponsorship: Women's Sports, 1982-2001', NCAA website: http://www.ncaa.org/index.

[121] https://www.ncsasports.org/womens-soccer/colleges
[122] '2001 Division I Men's Soccer Attendance', and 'Division I Women's Attendance', NCAA website: http://www.ncaa.org/index.
[123] NCAA Women's attendance, http://www.ncaa.org/stats/w_soccer/1/2006/2006_d1_w_soccer_attendance.pdf

and 2016 when USC played UCLA in front of a crowd of 10,128 and 8,508 spectators respectively demonstrating that in women's soccer, too, bitter rivalries draw crowds.[124] Yet the success of soccer for both genders at the college level should be kept in perspective when compared to intercollegiate football and basketball on the men's side, both significant occupants of the American cultural sports space. To give an example from my own University of Michigan: Whereas the men's football team draws over 100,000 spectators to its home games every Saturday during the football season, and the men's basketball team plays its home games in an arena with a seating capacity just shy of 14,000, barely 2,000 fans attend men's and women's varsity soccer games on a good day, with the men's team averaging just over 1,000 spectators per game in 2017.[125] The women's team averaged just over 850 spectators per game in 2016.[126] While some University of Michigan football, men's basketball, as well as hockey players are known and recognized all over the United States and Canada, soccer players (both male and female) are not even known on campus.

Additionally, women's basketball on the national level is generally much more popular and draws far more spectators on campus (and television viewers at home) than does soccer. Women's basketball programs such as the University of Connecticut's, the University of Tennessee's, Baylor University's, Notre Dame University's, the

---

[124] http://fs.ncaa.org/Docs/stats/w_soccer_RB/2017/Attendance.pdf
[125] http://fs.ncaa.org/Docs/stats/m_soccer_RB/2017/Attendance.pdf
[126] http://fs.ncaa.org/Docs/stats/w_soccer_RB/2017/Attendance.pdf

University of Louisville's, the University of North Carolina's, Duke University's, Stanford University's, the University of Texas's, the University of Maryland's and Rutgers University's – to name but the most prominent ones – have national recognition, with some of their players having become nationally known celebrities almost comparable to their male counterparts; moreover, women's intercollegiate volleyball and softball draw more spectators than women's soccer on America's campuses.

No presentation on women's soccer in the United States – particularly on the college level – could omit the unique role of the University of North Carolina, that legendary basketball school, whose women's soccer team amassed 22 national titles (one in the AIAW in 1981, that association's final year; and 21 in the NCAA out of a possible 37, having reached the final four in these 37 tournaments 28 times). These incredible numbers represent a rare and stellar achievement in any team sport, male or female, at the Division I level of college sports. Apart from the record winning streaks, record Final Four appearances, record most valuable players at NCAA tournaments, record Atlantic Coast Conference (ACC) championships, record national championships and many other unparalleled collective and individual accolades, the Tar Heels' true contribution to women's soccer in the United States has been their unique and direct influence on the United States women's national team. The Tar Heel tally on the United States national team includes: 43

different Carolina players on the roster of the United States National team since its inception; nine of the 18 players that won the first official and FIFA-sanctioned women's World Cup in 1991 in China plus the team's coach, Anson Dorrance; eight Tar Heels players on the victorious 1999 World Cup championship team and six Heels on the 2000 Olympic silver medal team in Sidney; and similar numbers on all subsequent US national teams that have thus far attained some sort of medal at all Olympics (excepting the one in Rio in 2016) and Women's World Cups. As of January 20, 2019, the current US Women's National Team features five former Tar Heels which is the most from any school on the team.[127] This squad will represent the United States at the Women's World Cup in France this upcoming summer. Above all, the world's best-known female soccer player of all time, perhaps the game's single true superstar on a global level, and a stalwart member of America's soccer successes from the late 1980s, actually, until the early 2000s, Mia Hamm, is a UNC graduate. It is to a brief discussion of the American national team that I now turn, which has been consistently and exclusively comprised of women who played soccer at American colleges. It's simple: no excellence in college soccer, no excellence on the national team in women's soccer. American college campuses have been the driving engine of the success of the American women's national team and thus of American women's soccer.

---

[127] https://www.ussoccer.com/womens-national-team/latest-roster#tab-1

The United States National Team: The Making of Global Leaders in an "Un-American" Sport

With women involved in the game at the recreational, scholastic, and college level to a degree unprecedented anywhere else in the world, American women became the very best in a sport in which the country's men – at least until the 2002 World Cup tournament in Japan and South Korea and not counting their semifinal appearance in the first tournament in 1930 – have remained mediocre on the global level though have had some regional success in the bi-annual CONCACAF tournament by winning six Gold Cups second only to Mexico's ten. Unlike any other team in the world, America's women's national soccer team has – almost incredibly -- medaled in twelve of the thirteen top-level global competitions in women's Association football since 1991: winner of the first World Cup in China in 1991; bronze medalist at the second World Cup in Sweden in 1995; winner and gold medalist at the Olympics in Atlanta in 1996, the first women's soccer tournament at the Olympic games; winner of the World Cup in the United States in 1999; silver medalist at the Olympics in Sidney in 2000; bronze medalist at the World Cup in the United States in 2003; winner and gold medalist at the Olympics in Athens in 2004; bronze medalist at the World Cup in China in 2007; gold medalist at the Beijing Olympics in 2008; silver medalist at the World Cup in Germany in 2011; winner and gold medalist at the 2012 Olympics in London; and winner of the World Cup in Canada in

2015. Only at the very last Olympics in Rio de Janeiro in 2016 did Team USA fail to medal by being eliminated in the quarterfinal by one of its main rivals, Sweden coached by Team USA's former manager Swedish great Pia Sundhage. Of the 18 women world-wide who have been capped by their respective countries more than 200 times, 11 have been American.

In addition to these most prestigious competitions in women's soccer, the United States national team has also been the most successful in the Algarve Cup often commonly though unofficially called the "Mini FIFA Women's World Cup". This competition comprises a global invitational tournament for national teams in women's soccer. Held annually in the Algarve region of Portugal since 1994 under the auspices of the Portuguese Football Federation (FPF), this annual tournament is one of the most prestigious women's soccer events, alongside the Women's World Cup and Women's Olympic Football. The twelve best women's national teams of the world are invited, with the top eight competing for the championship. The American women have won the tournament a record ten times, followed by four championships each for the Norwegians and the Swedes, with Germany possessing three, China two and Canada and Spain one each. The 2018 champions were the Dutch women who, in the previous year, also attained their first European championship. Clearly, the Algarve tournament's existence, and most certainly its importance, hails from the fact that on the women's side of Association football the competition by each country's national team far surpasses in prestige and significance the contests by its respective clubs. While women's club football's international importance has been steadily growing in Europe by the increasing popularity of the UEFA Champions League, the paucity in attendance at women's club matches as mentioned in the case of Germany and England – two of the sport's most ardent and pedigreed countries -- attests to the sport's continued weakness in terms of its popularity on the club side.

Above all, the 1999 World Cup tournament held in the United States created a moment when – for the very first time – the game enjoyed a genuine and broad popular following among the American public, as large numbers of Americans truly cared and followed this event to an extent hitherto unexperienced by soccer in the United States. The difference to the men's World Cup five years before was precisely the women's team's excellence and its real chance to win the tournament. Of course, the men's World Cup was a huge event. Indeed, it remains the most successful World Cup ever in terms of attendance at games and the paucity of troubling incidents. The American public attended all matches with enthusiasm (e.g. Morocco vs. Saudi Arabia on a Wednesday afternoon drawing nearly 77,000 spectators to Giants Stadium in the Meadowlands) which was based on curiosity and interest in witnessing an event that was singular in America's sports history. For the men's World Cup, the large public was an interested observer and a delighted participant in a mega event, but it never became passionately partisan since nobody expected the U.S. men's team to go deep into the tournament, let alone win it. Emerging from the group stage and losing respectably to Brazil on the Fourth of July in a crucial elimination game constituted an honorable showing for Team USA in the tournament of 1994.

With the women's event in 1999, the dimensions of public involvement were quite different in that the American public knew – and expected – that the women would contend for the title. Indeed, they were the clear favorites to win it. And they did not disappoint. Six special athletes, charismatic individuals and unquestioned pioneers of women's soccer all over the world – Michelle Akers, Brandy Chastain, Joy Fawcett, Julie Foudy, Kristine Lilly, and Mia Hamm -- led a group of young women to a special victory in front of more than 90,000 spectators at the venerable Rose Bowl in Pasadena including the President of the United States and millions of television viewers. Tellingly of women's position in this gendered world much beyond sports, the only thing remembered by a vast majority of the public about this fabulous nail-biter of a game -- against a superb Chinese team that was decided by penalty kicks after the overtime did not break a 0 – 0 tie -- was Brandi Chastain's taking off her jersey after scoring the winning penalty for the United States and running toward her teammates only in her bra.[128] Instead, fact is that – as the subtitle of Jere Longman's fine book about this tournament and its final match so aptly states – the United States women's national soccer team changed the world.[129]

Significantly, the success of the United States national team led directly to the establishment of the first venue for routinized professional women's soccer, the Women's United Soccer Association discussed below. In retrospect, it can be said that the winning ways of Team USA on the field and the overall sheen of the 1999 World Cup in garnering the interest and attention of the American public and media put women's soccer on the cultural map, carving out a recognizable – though small -- niche in America's sports space. Though not getting anywhere near the media attention devoted to either men's sports (such as the Big Four of baseball, football, basketball and hockey; but also soccer) or individual women's sports (most notably tennis, figures skating and gymnastics), the American national team had drawn decent numbers of spectators to some games prior to the 1999 tournament, such as a 1997 match between the United States and England in San Jose, California, that attracted a crowd of over seventeen thousand.[130] But it was the 1999 World Cup that engendered a newly found popularity and respect for women's soccer far beyond the confines of recreational activity or a

---

[128] Brandi Chastain, *It's Not About the Bra: How to Play Hard, Play Fair, and Put the Fun Back into Competitive Sports* (New York: HarperCollins, 2004).
[129] Jere Longman, *The Girls of Summer: The U.S. Women's Soccer Team and How It Changed the World* (New York: HarperCollins, 2000).
[130] US Soccer Federation, *US Soccer Federation Media Guide*, 1998, p. 12.

small number of spectator enthusiasts for the college game. This victory at the Rose Bowl affected culture.

As noted above, all the United States national team's players were then – and have been since -- products of the nation's college soccer. The fact that women playing team sports at the professional level now represents an acceptable and positive development for most Americans highlights the progress made in the United States for gender equality. It also accentuates the differences between the ways in which both the game of soccer and sports played by women are perceived in the United States in comparison to most other nations, particularly where soccer and its overwhelmingly male culture dominate the sports space. Julie Foudy, retired midfielder for Team USA (and in the meantime one of the country's most respected women leaders and perhaps the most outspoken advocate of the continued existence of Title IX as the corner stone for women's sports and women's rights in team sports and well beyond in the United States), stated the essential difference between soccer's gendered world in the United States and much of the rest of the world quite clearly: 'Everyone plays soccer here [in the United States]. Girls are encouraged. But you travel abroad, and the game is considered a man's world in so many cultures. A girl is considered a freak if she plays. We've been to Spain and jumped into a men's game and been looked at like we were crazy'.[131]

---

[131] Harvey Araton, 'A Pioneer in Her Sport and Beyond', *The New York Times*, 28 July 1998, C23. The contrast regarding the perception of women's soccer in the US on the one hand and that found in Europe and Latin America on the other was striking: Most media in the latter regions ignored the 1999 World Women's Cup or gave it

Perhaps most impressive of all, Team USA attracted media coverage – which started slowly and steadily increased toward the crescendo of the final, then gradually subsided over the next two weeks – that could easily rival what is routinely directed at the Big Four. The attention which the women soccer players garnered in one month far surpassed all the cumulative media coverage attained by MLS in its entire three-year existence up to that time. Each night of the tournament, late night television talk-show host David Letterman displayed a photo of the women's national team in which all twenty players appeared to be wearing nothing but Late Show t-shirts. Letterman himself transformed the term 'soccer moms' into the racier and more risqué 'soccer mamas' and the openly sexualized 'soccer babes', highlighting an aspect of women's team sports heretofore avoided or actually suppressed: An image of femininity and wholesome sexual appeal purveyed as a message "that women can be both athletic and feminine in an endeavor that, in many countries, still carries the stigma that women who play are somehow unwomanly". Indeed, a side-angle photo of Team USA defender Brandi Chastain "crouched behind a soccer ball wearing only her cleats and her rippling muscles", drew the attention of journalists, pundits, and reporters, as well as many people with little previous interest in soccer.[132]

---

marginal coverage at best. German television, for example, broadcast only the second half of the US-China final (commencing at 11 PM local time), preferring instead to air its usual late-night Saturday soccer talk show featuring an off-season interview with the coach of a Bundesliga club.

[132] Jere Longman, 'Pride in Their Play, and in Their Bodies', *The New York Times*, 8 July 1999, D1, D4. When

Here we are at one of the absolute key differences between men's and women's sports, namely the de rigueur and inevitable sexualization of the latter. This phenomenon is best exemplified by what one could call the "Anna Kournikova effect," in which an athlete who had been a very good though not an exceptional super-star-caliber player on the women's professional tennis tour still became and continues to remain – solely by dint of her beauty – an absolute global celebrity and a household name.[133] During a panel discussion in 2011, Lindsey Van, the female American ski jumper who led the successful campaign to get the International Olympic Committee to include women's (not just men's, as was previously the case) ski jumping in the Winter Olympic Games, said plainly, "You might not want to be known as the pretty naked girl ... but if you want to just be known for being good at your sport, you need to get attention in some other way first." She added, sounding somewhat frustrated, "Think about it: Famous female athletes are all beautiful. If you're a guy, all you need is to be the best. You don't need to do anything else. If you're a woman, to get attention, you have

Chastain threw off her shirt – to reveal a sports bra – after scoring the clincher in the final's shoot-out, some speculated that this was either an act of wanton exhibitionism, an instant of "momentary insanity" (as Chastain herself claimed), a ploy for gender equality (as shirt shedding by male players in celebration of a victorious moment was something of a tradition in soccer at the time, meanwhile banned), or a shrewd and calculated marketing ploy, since the sports bra in question was a Nike prototype planned for mass production. See Richard Sandomir, 'Was Sports Bra Celebration Spontaneous?', *The New York Times*, 8 July 1999, p. S6; and Melanie Welds and Ann Oldenburg, 'Sports Bra's Flash Could Cash In', *USA Today*, 13 July 1999, p. 2A.

[133] Michael Ventre, "'Kournikova Effect' Can Derail or Boost Athlete," NBVspots.com, February 26, 2007, available at http://nbcsports.msnbc.com/id/17203733/ns/sports// Anna Kournikova surely possessed immense athletic talent; in 1997, at age sixteen, she advanced all the way to the semifinals at Wimbledon, losing to that year's champion, Martina Hingis. Kournikova reached a number one Women's Tennis Association (WTA) ranking as a doubles player. With Martina Hingis as her partner, Anna Kournikova won two Grand Slam titles in women's doubles, both in Melbourne, in 1999 and 2002.

to be good at your sports *and* be beautiful. You can't just be good."[134] Conversely, it is very unlikely in any men's sport that a fine though not stellar athlete with no major achievements on the field would mutate into a sex symbol of global proportions off it and attain greater attention (and retain it well after his retirement from the sport) even than many a superstar with a distinguished record between the lines.

Moreover, lesbianism among female athletes has emerged into the open to the point where there are few stigmata or sanctions attached to it at the present time. This massive cultural shift has been relatively recent. Just think how Billie Jean King lost millions of dollars in endorsements when in 1981 she admitted to having had a lesbian affair. Now there is solid acceptability of, even display of pride in the lesbianism of many women athletes in team sports such as soccer and basketball, as well as in individual sports such as tennis and golf. Tellingly, gay men are still buried deep in the sports closet. With the exception of divers, gymnasts and figure skaters – arguably, the least macho sports in the public's eye and not associated with teams – no major athlete of the NBA, the NFL, the NHL or MLB has ever declared himself "outed" as gay during his days as an active player.[135] There is, of course, the exception of Robbie

---

[134] Lindsey Van, panel discussion at the Association of Women in Sports Media conference, June 25, 2011.
[135] There is, of course, the important memoir by British basketball player John Amaechi, who played in the NBA for five seasons with the Cleveland Cavaliers, the Orlando Magic, and the Utah Jazz, who chronicled his life as a closeted gay man in the NBA. The book, *Man in the Middle*, was published in 2007 and received some attention, especially Amaechi's chronicling of the intense hostility that he faced at the hand of the Jazz's head coach Jerry Sloan, though this was due to Sloan's disrespect for Amaechi's modest basketball abilities rather than his homophobia. Of course, Amaechi describes how the entire locker room culture in the NBA was openly homophobic but he also gives credit to many of his fellow players who – though never explicitly acknowledging Amaechi's gayness – seem to have been tacitly aware of his sexual orientation. The point however remains: Amaechi was at best a role player, not anywhere near of having had star status in the League, *and* he published his memoirs after his

Rogers who, upon his returning home to the United States from his playing days in England and being signed by the LA Galaxy in 2013, declared publicly his being gay thus becoming the very first male athlete of any major American team sports to do so. No offense to MLS and its rising importance but its standing in America's public eye and quotidian life still has not attained the heights enjoyed by the NFL, NBA, NHL and MLB thus making Rogers' brave coming out perhaps a tad less risky than it would have been for a player active in those four leagues. The exact same thing pertains to football in its culturally hegemonic spaces of Europe and Latin America thus rendering football the exact cultural equivalent to the Big Four North American team sports. Virtually no players in either have ever declared themselves gay during their playing days.[136]

The soccer players of the women's 1999 team furnished the cover stories for *Time, Newsweek,* and *Sports Illustrated* the week after the final. They also graced the cover of *People* magazine (with glowing personal profiles of all eleven starters inside) the following week. Public appearances of the full squad after the tournament -- at Disneyland, the Women's National Basketball Association (WNBA) All-Star game, on

playing days were over. Amaechi was later joined by Jason Collins who came out about being gay while still playing in the NBA though very much towards the end of his career. One needs to mention the University of Missouri's football player Michael Sam in this context adding the fact that despite being a star defensive player for his school, Sam never made it to the NFL. There are a few individuals who, as players in culturally hegemonic male-dominated team sports declared themselves publicly as gay during their playing days. They are Ian Roberts in Rugby League; Gareth Thomas, a rare dual player in Rugby League and Rugby Union; and Steven Davies in cricket.

[136] I would be remiss not to alert the reader to Justinus Soni "Justin" Fashanu, the English footballer of Nigerian descent who came out in 1990. Even though the abuse he suffered from his teammates and fellow footballers after his announcement was, according to him, tolerable; the derision from the fans was nothing short of brutal and shameful. Fashanu was doubly abused during his playing days: for being gay and black.

NBC television's Today Show (and outside the studio), at the White House meeting President Bill Clinton (who had attended two tournament matches, including the final) – all rated high profile coverage in both the sports and main news sections of nearly all American daily newspapers and on local television news shows, as well as on the ubiquitous Cable News Network (CNN). All these developments bespoke qualities of consumed culture that go well beyond the confines of the (mostly indifferent) public perception usually accorded to women's team sports, or soccer as a recreational or viewer activity in the United States at the time. Indeed, the players of Team USA had achieved – at least for a few weeks -- the rarity of 'crossover stardom', a status attained by only a few select athletes of the Big Four.

Perhaps most significantly, the US team's most prominent members – Julie Foudy, Brandi Chastain, Mia Hamm, Kristine Lilly, Michelle Akers, Joy Fawcett and Briana Scurry (the goalie, and the only African American member of the starting eleven) -- became nationally known sports figures and heroes. They were role models for millions of young American girls who aspired to be soccer players and athletes in other sports. Several of these Team USA players netted lucrative sponsorship and promotional deals; Hamm, specifically, became a regular star in television commercials and magazine advertisements often featured together with Michael Jordan, the ultimate global crossover superstar. Hamm's media presence lasted well past her retirement as an active player in 2006.

It is not an exaggeration to say that the success of the American women's national team in 1999 and the attention accorded the World Cup tournament that year provided the initial impetus for what could conceivably become a long and fruitful though, as we will see, also rocky history of women's professional soccer on the club level in the United States and, perhaps, the world. The exceptional success of the American women's game on the level of the national team fulfills two key conditions essential to making any sport popular in the United States or, for that matter, anywhere else. The first is attractiveness for being the very best (i.e., quality as a means). The other is attractiveness for winning and making the fans feel proud of being American in a sport where being American had not been a major source of pride and satisfaction (i.e., quality as an end). And though a successful Women's World Cup was not a sufficient condition for the establishment of a women's professional soccer league in the United States, it most definitely constituted a necessary one. Such a league was indeed established, beginning play in the spring of 2001.

The Ups and Downs of Professionalization: The Women's United Soccer Association (WUSA); Women's Professional Soccer (WPS) and the National Women's Soccer League (NWSL)

Women's soccer may present an opportunity to utilize what I have termed the optimality syndrome also known as the "best of the best" that has been a key requisite for the successful perpetuation of any team sport and major league in the American sports space.[137] To wit: It is a given for Americans (as well as for sports fans in the rest of the world) that Major League Baseball, the National Football League, the National Basketball Association, and the National Hockey League all represent the ultimate in their respective sports. Indeed, athletes in any of the Big Four from anywhere in the world must by necessity aspire to play in these North American venues if they want to compete and play with the best of the best. Yet, the situation for soccer on the men's side has been exactly the opposite. The best of the best, including a fair number of Americans, play in Europe.

The international structure of sports, like much else, can well be explained in what political sociologists have called "center-periphery" or "core-periphery" relations. In this arrangement, the center (or core) sets the dominant tone in defining the sport's parameters such as its rules and fields of activity and culture well beyond the playing grounds proper.

[137] See Markovits and Hellerman, *Offside*, pp. 159-161. Though another American exception, this aspect of American team sports is mostly an outgrowth of their development in relative geographic isolation in the era (1870-1930) I have identified as crucial to the establishment of modern hegemonic sports culture.

The core features the best players and clubs, its contests are not only coveted at home but also elsewhere, including the peripheries. Typically, all players in the peripheries who want to make it in the sport and – most important – earn the most money for their talents can only do so in the core. Conversely, players who have excelled in the core and are on a declining trajectory in their careers often seek out employment in the peripheries.

In the Big Four North American team sports, there can be no doubt that the United States and Canada furnish the uncontested global core. All great European and Latin American basketball players want to play in the NBA which is the ultimate measure of their success. Ditto with Russian, Czech, Slovak, Finnish, Swedish and German hockey players: they all migrate to the NHL. Yes, Russia has the Kontinental Hockey League (KHL) which is home to some excellent players and offers first-rate quality hockey. But until the likes of Alex Ovechkin and Evgeni Malkin play in the NHL and Canadian stars like Sidney Crosby and Connor McDavid or their American colleagues Patrick Kane and Jack Eichel do not even consider playing in the KHL, let alone go there, it is evident that the core of the sport's top level resides on the left side of the Atlantic not its right. MLB also represents baseball's core. The best Dominican, Puerto Rican and Venezuelan but also Japanese and Korean players seek to play in North America with American players in their fading years seeking employment in Japan or elsewhere. The NFL is a bit of an exception to this arrangement since American football, though nominally played in many countries of the world that compete for a World Cup of American Football on a regular basis, remains a virtually all-American affair in which there essentially is no periphery. Thus, it is not by chance that of the four North American sports leagues, the NFL is far and away the most local and parochial, the least international and cosmopolitan when it comes to its players' origins.

The structure of American men's soccer is exactly the obverse of the one just described for the Big Four team sports. Here, the United States has been on the periphery to Western and Southern Europe's core. The best American players such as the country's exquisite goal keepers like Brad Friedel, Kasey Keller, Tim Howard and Brad Guzan all found employment in perhaps the soccer core's pinnacle: the English Premier League and the German Bundesliga. Some of America's premier field players like Brian McBride, Clint Dempsey, Alexi Lalas, and Landon Donovan also played in the game's core in Europe. At the time of this writing, the great hope of American men's soccer – Christian Pulisic – has developed into a star with the prestigious German club Borussia Dortmund which he is about to leave for arguably an even stouter denizen of the game's core: Chelsea Football Club in West London. The tension perennially present in all core-periphery relations came to the fore on the men's side when Jürgen Klinsmann, the former coach of the men's national team, berated some American soccer players for not honing their skills properly by taking employment in the American soccer periphery instead of the European football core.

On the men's side there exists an added obstacle for being from Association football's periphery trying to succeed in its core: the burden of newness, a well-known concept to economists, coupled with the burden of being American in a world where American power has been reluctantly – for lack of a better alternative -- accepted often coupled with a massive disdain for aspects of America as an uncouth and uncultured place.[138] Male American footballers have had the hardest time being accepted by their European peers and have confronted an animosity that players of other peripheral countries never did. Precisely by dint of being the core of most everything in the 20th century – including sports, of course – America's peripheral standing in soccer throughout this time became an irritant to Europeans precisely when the United States began to move from periphery to semi- periphery in this sport on its way to reaching its core at some point in the not-to-distant future. One could handle a giant who in one part of culture – in this case football – remained an irrelevant minnow. But leaving that sphere of marginality by hosting the World Cup in 1994 and becoming a major force in many aspects of the game (ownership of some of the most coveted clubs in the world, becoming the largest contingent of World Cup soccer fans traveling to the venues etc. etc.) America deeply

---

[138] I have studied the presence of anti-Americanism in many aspects of European public life, not least that of sports. For more details, please see Andrei S. Markovits, *Uncouth Nation: Why Europe Dislikes America* (Princeton: Princeton University Press, 2007)

annoyed members of the core. Hating the big and successful has always been acceptable in sport. Just ask the New York Yankees, the New England Patriots, the Los Angeles Lakers, Duke basketball, Manchester United, Real Madrid, Juventus or Bayern Munich to name just a few much-hated bigs! But nothing engenders deeper hatred and more contempt than a nouveau riche, a parvenu, a newcomer who lacks tradition and thus appears to be fake, pushy, illegitimate but most important, threatening. Just ask RB Leipzig in the German Bundesliga![139] And the Schadenfreude directed at a ubiquitously powerful agent in a realm in which it is weak feels particularly good and rewarding. And super power America's rare existence as a minnow in Association football has been a major irritant in Europe. Damned if you do, damned if you don't: On the one hand, Europeans are irritated about the fact that otherwise mighty America has been so unimportant and even disinterested in their beloved football. On the other hand, once America attempts to join this world, it is perceived as distorting, inauthentic but above all threatening. Whereas it has become socially unacceptable to deride and ridicule a weak player on the global scene, it remains completely acceptable, indeed laudable, to do so towards the strong. Nowhere has this contempt for America's connection to soccer been more pronounced than in England where the very word "soccer", an English term which was indeed used with some frequency in the world

---

[139] See Pavel Brunssen's superb MA Thesis written at the Technical University in Berlin. Pavel Brunssen, "'Niemals ein Teil des Spiels': Antisemitische Ressentimentkommunikation gegen RB Leipzig in den Fußball-Fanszenen der Bundesrepublik Deutschland" (Berlin: Technical University Berlin, unpublished MA Thesis, 2018).

of English football precisely until the emergence of the United States from its previous position in the unthreatening periphery to becoming an intruder in the core over the past three decades, has become a blasphemous expression encountering nothing but hatred, rage and contempt.[140] All foreign accents have become acceptable in English football with one exception: American English! A prominent case that stands for many others: Bob Bradley, the former long-time coach of the United States Men's National Team attempting to deploy his managerial (coaching) skills in the English Premier League. "It is Bradley's nationality that condemns him. Danny Gabbidon, a former Wales international, said on the radio after the game that the accent of Bradley, a New Jersey native, meant that he 'could not take him seriously.'"[141] No other nationality invites the negative scrutiny in English football that is accorded as a matter of course to Americans. Indeed, to some football fans in Europe, the prowess of the American women in this sport has served as another item in the vast array of prima facie evidence for how the despised Yanks have sullied the sanctity of this glorious game and its culture.

But none of this exists in the women's game. For women's soccer, a venue emerged after the 1999 World Cup triumph that fulfilled the requisite of representing the best of the best in the American sports

---

[140] See Stefan Szymanski und Silke-Maria Weineck, *It's Football, Not Soccer (And Vice Versa): On the History, Emotion and Ideology Behind One of the Internet's Most Ferocious Debates* (2018)
[141] Rory Smith, "Romance Turns Sour for Swansea Fans, and Bob Bradley Is Caught in the Middle," *The New York Times, November 6, 2016.*

space and constituting the United States as women's soccer global core: the Women's United Soccer Association, a league in which not only the best American players competed, but also to which the top women soccer players from all over the world migrated. Thus, WUSA could have possibly redefined how women's team sports and their participants were perceived and valued by American society (and, perhaps, by other nations as well). It was not to be.

The WUSA was founded in the spring of 2000 by John Hendricks, Chairman and Chief Executive Officer (CEO) of Discovery Communications, along with other high-profile corporate investors such as Cox Communications, Time Warner Cable, and Comcast Corporation. With an initial stake of $40 million, the plan was to make the league profitable – or at least self-sufficient -- within five years.[142] Like MLS, the WUSA was organized and funded as a "single entity business structure". Rather than owning individual franchises linked through confederation (as found in the Big Four in North America and most professional sports leagues throughout the world), "club operators owned a financial stake in the league, not just their individual team", while player contracts were owned by the league, not the teams.[143] Prior to reaching an accommodation with MLS executives who had their own plans for a professional women's league, the brand new WUSA signed all twenty players from the world champion American national team,

---

[142] WUSA Communications Department, *WUSA 2002 Official Media Guide*, p. 6, 8.
[143] Ibid, p. 21.

designating each a 'founding player' awarded with equity shares in the league.[144] Player salaries in the WUSA were set at a yearly minimum of $27,000 and a maximum of $85,000. The league consisted of eight teams located throughout the United States (Atlanta, Boston, Carolina, New York, Philadelphia, San Diego, San Jose, and Washington, D.C.), with each team playing a 22-game season from April through August. A four-team playoff culminated in the Founders Cup league championship (won by San Jose in 2001, Carolina in 2002, and Boston in 2003).[145] As noted, the WUSA provided the forum for the best of women's soccer from both the United States and the rest of the world. It really formed the global core of women's soccer for a brief time. Thus, nine players from China were on WUSA rosters for 2002, while some of the league's top performers – including Hege Riise (Norway), Birgit Prinz (Germany) and Marinette Pichon (France) who won the Most Valuable Player and Offensive Player of the Year awards in 2002 – hailed from outside the United States.[146] "Up to four international players were allowed on each squad and provided an example of a core of activity attracting migrant groups of players from the stronger elite countries and individual talents from others. Though it was primarily intended to provide professional employment for United States national team

---

[144] See Markovits and Hellerman, *Offside*, pp. 180-181; and *WUSA 2002 Official Media Guide*, p. 32. Nineteen of the twenty players from the Team USA's 1999 World Cup roster played in the WUSA. Michelle Akers retired soon after the 1999 tournament but was still awarded a financial stake in the league.
[145] Paul Dodson, WUSA Manager of Sports Communications, personal communication, 19 November 2002.
[146] WUSA Communications Department, *WUSA 2002 Official Media Guide*, p. 34. "Best of the Best," *Soccer America*, 57, 18 (9 September 2002), 33.

players, the league also aimed to be a breakthrough for women's football world-wide. For a brief three seasons, it did achieve that goal."[147] Thus, the WUSA had indeed fulfilled the requirements for attracting the best of the best in the world while also utilizing the public's identification with the success of American athletes on the world stage.

But playing and following soccer – and women's soccer specifically– are two completely different things. And the chasm between activity (production, i.e. playing) and culture (consumption, i.e. following) remained pronounced in the case of the WUSA. Attendance figures at matches and television ratings declined from the league's first season to its second, as expenses far exceeded the initial $40 million seed, reportedly by close to double at the end of 2002.[148] To cut costs, the WUSA reduced roster sizes from 20 to 18 players and moved its league offices from New York to Atlanta.[149] Average attendance per match dipped from 8,104 for 2001 to 6,957 for 2002; a total of 585,374 spectators attended 84 matches in 2002, with a high of 24,000 at RFK Stadium in Washington, D.C., on July 7 to a low of 4,002 at Mitchell

---

[147] Jean Williams, "Women's Football, Europe and Professionalization, 1971 – 2011", Research Report, International Centre for Sports History and Culture, De Montford University, 2012; pp. 36, 37. https://www.dora.dmu.ac.uk/bitstream/handle/2086/5806/Woman%27s%20football%2C%20Europe%20%26%20pr ofessionalization%201971-2011.pdf?sequence=1&isAllowed=y. This study was later published under the title *Globalising Women's Football: Europe, Migration and Professionalization* (Bern: Peter Lang, 2013).
[148] Scott French, WUSA: 'Profitable by 2007? Increased revenues spark hope as attendance, TV ratings decline', *Soccer America*, 57, 18 (9 September 2002), 35. Though WUSA officials say expenses have declined by 28 percent, league founder John Hendricks said that 'the league will have spent, by the end of 2002, $75 million-$80 million in total. (In addition, $24 million was spent on stadium development.)' According to Hendricks, the balance between revenues and expenses was approximately $20 million. 'That would make for revenues of about $9 million in 2002 and $5.5 million in 2001. Doing the math, WUSA investors have lost about $55 million since the league's formation'.
[149] Michelle Smith and Dwight Chapin, 'WUSA is gearing for seconds'. *San Francisco Chronicle*, 13 April 2002, C3.

Field in New York (Uniondale, Long Island) on July 20.[150] To be sure, these were – and still are – excellent numbers when compared to the attendance figures that we encountered in the section discussing women's club football in England and Germany. Indeed, these WUSA figures were on average the highest spectator numbers for women's club soccer in the world.

With the exception of specific events such as the World Cup, the European National Championships and the Champions League Final matches in recent years constituting the most pronounced evidence for what I have discussed above as the "Olympianization" of American soccer, "regular" i.e. club-level soccer of any variety – including men's – has continued to be a tough sell to an American television audience as evidenced by MLS's low television ratings which, in the meantime, have been partially offset by the growing attendance at games that have attained global respectability. Anybody witnessing the MLS Cup final match between the Portland Timber and a barely one-year old Atlanta United Football Club in front of more than 73,000 spectators in Atlanta's Mercedes-Benz Stadium in early December 2018 must realize that soccer in the United States has come a long way from its former marginality. While still not close to the levels of cultural relevance owned by baseball, basketball and American football (though perhaps approaching that of hockey), there can be no question that men's soccer

---

[150] Paul Dodson, WUSA Manager of Sports Communications, personal communication, 19 November 2002.

– even on the club level – has attained a level of respectability in the United States. By many dimensions – most crucially atmospherics – the MLS Cup final match could have occurred in any of the sport's core cities in England, Germany, Italy or Spain. Indeed, six weeks later, the same venue housed Super Bowl LIII with the atmosphere inside the stadium being in no way more electric or knowledgeable or involved than it was during MLS Cup.

But the world of soccer in the America of the early 2000s was still very different from what it came to be nearly two decades later. It should be no surprise then that the ratings for cable broadcasts of WUSA games were quite low, though the decline of 75 percent from the first season (0.4 on Turner Network Television and the now-defunct CNN-Sports Illustrated) to 2002 (0.1 on PAX TV) could be viewed as precipitous and foreboding.[151] At the end of 2002, the league's solvency remained contingent on the willingness of Hendricks (openly and affectionately called 'St. John' by WUSA players) to provide the funds necessary to maintain operations.[152] But even this honorific sainthood bestowed on Hendricks could not save the WUSA. At the end of the 2003 season, he called a press conference to declare the end of this short-lived experiment. With losses close to $100 million, the league had become untenable.

---

[151] Scott French, WUSA: 'Profitable by 2007? Increased revenues spark hope as attendance, TV ratings decline', *Soccer America*, 57, 18 (9 September 2002), 35.
[152] George Vecsey, 'W.U.S.A. Recognizes Its New Talent Amid Thanks for "St. John",' *The New York Times*, 25 August 2002, p. SP8.

The WUSA's own research revealed that 66 percent of its "fan base" (those attending at least one game) was female in 2001, and 70 percent was in 2002.[153] Additionally, the league's demographic analysis also demonstrated that nearly 30 percent of those attending its games were under the age of fifteen, mostly girls accompanied by older family members (more than 50 percent of whom had an annual income of at least $80,000).[154] Demographic data of the television audience for the 1999 Women's World Cup showed that prior to the final (when the television audience just about broke even by gender) "women comprised only 34 percent of the World Cup audience on ESPN and 35 percent on ESPN 2, compared with 39 percent for ESPN's WNBA games and 40 percent for the NCAA women's basketball championship tournament".[155] (Indeed, these figures for women's basketball reveal something of a weakness in the female fan base for that sport as well.) While virtually every expert agrees that the WUSA was poorly managed, especially in its insistence to remain separate from the men's game and its prime purveyor of Major League Soccer, the league's failure surely corroborated the reality of soccer's growing but still precarious presence in America's sports culture. Just because millions produce a sport does not mean that they also will consume it. Just because millions bowl, run, swim, fish in no way means that millions will watch these sports on

---

[153] WUSA Communications Department, *WUSA 2002 Official Media Guide*, p. 170; and 'The Smart Way to Reach America's Families', WUSA promotional kit, 2002.

[154] 'The Smart Way to Reach America's Families'.

[155] Richard Sandomir, 'Sale of Cup Merchandise Just Didn't Take Off', *The New York Times*, 13 July 1999, p. D4.

television or live at the venues even if performed by professionals. There is a major chasm between "doing" and "following" a sport – and nowhere is this more pronounced than among women. A fundamental change in the way most women and girls relate to team sports needs to occur should the "following" become a larger and more robust phenomenon. There needs to be a change from the activity of recreation and participation to a culture of spectatorship, following, and affect (if not exactly the same as what is found in the hegemonic sports culture that is overwhelmingly male, then some sort of variation involving significant numbers of females) in order for a women's team sport (soccer in this case) to become a truly significant player in the American sports space. In this aspect, the United States most certainly offers no exception when compared to all other comparable countries of the democratic West. Indeed, this is the same in every society: Women have yet to create a team sport that has entered that society's hegemonic sports culture. Of course, this has not been the case in individual sports such as figure skating, tennis, skiing, swimming and track and field, where many individual women have indeed very much become part of certain countries' – and the world's -- hegemonic sports culture. Just think of Katharina Witt, the Williams sisters, Steffi Graf, Lindsey Vonn, Wilma Rudolph, Jackie Joyner Kersey, Nadia Comaneci, on and on to mention just a few.

Still, the WUSA was not all for naught. A successor league called Women's Professional Soccer (WPS) commenced play in the spring of 2009. Fielding teams in metropolitan Boston, Chicago, Dallas, Los Angeles, New York, St. Louis, the San Francisco Bay Area and Washington, D.C. these eight teams comprised a new professional women's soccer league that consciously and conscientiously aimed to avoid WUSA's missteps. Thus, in contrast to WUSA, which employed a top-down model by relying on star players alone who, so the league hoped, would earn it quick profits, WPS opted to pursue a local, grass roots approach "from below" that emphasized slow and steady growth. Still, some of the world's very best female soccer players joined this league arguably making it – just like WUSA before it -- the very best forum for women's soccer on the globe.

Not only did WPS draft many of the top players from the United States national team and dispersed them strategically among the eight participating teams, but so were four of the best Japanese female soccer players and ten of the very best Brazilian players, including superstar Marta who played in Los Angeles but also returned to her native Brazil during WPS's off season to join Pele's old club Santos where she was accorded the immense honor of wearing Pele's coveted number 10 jersey. Marta became the very first woman to play on a man's team, which, even if a gimmick, was arguably the most powerful testimony as to how far women's soccer had come in the world if a woman was given a spot on a man's team in a decidedly macho sport in an equally macho society wearing the sport's most iconic and coveted number on her jersey: 10! Marta's Brazilian compatriots Daniela joined St. Louis and Cristiane played in Chicago, adding to the increasingly cosmopolitan and diverse line-ups of women's soccer in the United States. The aforementioned best English female footballer and Arsenal star Kelly Smith commenced play in Boston.

Despite all this careful planning and attracting all this national and international talent, by the end of the first season -- in which the New York area-based Sky Blue FC won the championship – several of the league's teams lost twice as much revenue as expected ranging between $1 million to $2 million. This was largely due to these teams' inability to attract local sponsors even though global sporting goods manufacturer Puma committed itself to invest in the league. The league's average per-game attendance came to 4,500 fans, about what its executives had anticipated. Despite these uneven results, WPS was on track to expand to nine teams in 2010 with franchises in Atlanta and Philadelphia.[156]

WPS eventually folded and gave way to the newest venture into professional women's soccer, the National Women's Soccer League (NWSL), run by the United States Soccer Federation (USSF). Founded in 2012, with play beginning in 2013, the NWSL originally featured eight teams, four of which were carried over from the WPS. Since 2013,

---

[156] Ken Belson, "Women's League Seeks Sponsors" in *The New York Times*, August 25, 2009.

the league has expanded and added teams in Orlando and Houston, but it also lost a former WPS team in the Boston Breakers. FC Kansas City folded in 2017, after a change in ownership. All player contracts were transferred over to a new team, Utah Royals FC thus bringing the current team total to nine.

At the league's foundation, it was decided that players would come from the United States, Mexico, and Canada with them being evenly allocated among the 8 new teams. The initial salary cap per team was set at $500,000 which was significantly lower than that of the former WPS teams. This number was lowered still to $200,000 before the start of the 2013 season.[157] As of the 2018 season, this cap amount was increased to $350,000. Teams had to have a minimum of 18 players on their rosters, with room for 20 players maximum at any point during the season.[158] As of 2017, Mexico no longer allocates players to the NWSL, as the country founded its own professional women's league, called "Liga MX Femenil."

The NWSL has now played six seasons with the parity among the teams being quite successful in that there have been a number of champions. Four different teams have claimed the NWSL title with Portland Thorns FC and the former FC Kansas City each winning two titles. The average attendance at games in 2013 was just over 4,000. Average spectatorship per game grew to just over 6,000 in 2018,

---

[157] https://www.nytimes.com/2013/04/14/sports/soccer/national-womens-soccer-league-to-begin-play.html
[158] http://www.nwslsoccer.com/2017-roster-rules

showing that there is a market and a demand for professional women's soccer in the United States. [159] One city loves its team more than any other NWSL city: Portland, Oregon which, of course, has also become an enthusiastic supporter of its men's club, the Portland Timbers.

To wit: Between 2013 and 2016, average attendance for Portland Thorns FC games was over 13,000 which constitutes a phenomenal number for women's club soccer anywhere in the world. The team topped this impressive attendance rate in 2017 with over 17,000 people per game.[160] The next highest club average attendance in the United States in 2017 was 6,000 spectators. Putting this amazing record into perspective is the fact that some NWSL teams can barely manage to get over 1,000 people to games, yet the Thorns have never dipped below 13,000. It would not be erroneous to declare Portland, Oregon as the global success story and epicenter of women's soccer on the club level. Very impressive indeed! Fans of women's soccer, and soccer in the United States in general, can only hope that the city of Portland represents a welcome cultural vanguard for the sport.

[159] https://www.oregonlive.com/portland-thorns/2016/11/nwsl_saw_rising_attendance_num.html
[160] https://soccerstadiumdigest.com/2017-nwsl-attendance/

CONCLUSION

An Agent of Cosmopolitanism, Democratization and Inclusion: Feminization and the Transatlantic Rise of Women's Soccer in America and Women's Football in Europe

There can be no doubt that the phenomenal rise of women's presence in the game of Association Football on both sides of the Atlantic has been a mainstay in the altered world of sport over the past four decades. Both in Europe and in the United States, the trajectory of the women's game and its timeline have been nearly identical. Thanks to the massive social and cultural shifts caused by the so called second wave of feminism commencing in the late 1960s and early 1970s, women's soccer in the United States and women's football in Europe left their respective ghettoes of semi-official existence and transformed themselves from a curiosity and chicanery to a mainstay on the production side of team sports. Very few, if any, American and European women played this game in the late 1960s and early 1970s. But many millions do today. Case closed!

If the content of this change was virtually identical on both sides of the Atlantic, the form in which it happened could not have been more different. Both journeys were fraught with obstacles and difficulties of a differing nature. On the one hand, American women had it much easier than their European counterparts because they blazed a trail as soccer's pioneers and players in American sports history in a game that men had known but had traveled lightly to put it euphemistically. Furthermore, America's sports-obsessed men were not particularly interested nor especially invested in terms of their identity and culture in the existence of this soccer path. Precisely because soccer has had a subordinate position in the history of America's male-dominated hegemonic sports cultures was the path for women to succeed in this game much easier because unlike their European sisters, they did not have to enter an already occupied space and contest it against much opposition, derision and ridicule. Thus, on the important count of not having to contend with men in gaining a meaningful presence in soccer, the American women had a more facile journey than the Europeans to succeed and excel in this new world. On the other hand, one could also argue that the American women confronted an even more formidable task than their European counterparts in that the latter entered a structure and learned a language that had flourished in every European culture for nearly a century, whereas the former were pioneers in the very establishment of such a structure and language in the United States. In sum, the American women became trailblazers for a sport that itself had only led a marginal existence in American sport history as opposed to the European situation in which the women merely affirmed an already extant culture and language.

In comparing the different paths on these two continents regarding their respective costs and benefits, one could possibly make the argument that the American trajectory of not having to contest with men was more beneficial in the short run as demonstrated by the almost instant success of the women soccer players and their rise to international prominence. The reason that this least-resistance hypothesis might have some validity is best demonstrated by the fact that the women's game in China, the two Koreas, Denmark, Sweden, Norway, Canada, Australia and Japan flourished early on as well. In none of these countries did the men ever attain any degree of sustained success in Association football, despite Sweden's second place finish at the World Cup in 1958 in which the Swedes were the host nation, its third-place finish at the World Cup in 1994 played in the United States; and Denmark's winning the European Championship in 1992. Thus, I argue that at the earliest stages of the establishment of women's soccer, at its entrance into the sports space as it were, a relatively meek presence of the men's game might have been advantageous for the women's. However, as time passed and the women's game became more fully institutionalized, prowess and excellence in the men's game might have indeed infiltrated the women's. It is not by chance, I would argue, that the new international powers in women's football – joining the United States at the very top -- are Germany, Brazil, France and England (with the rapid rise of Mexico, Argentina, Spain and Italy), arguably among the most pedigreed and successful countries in the history of the men's game.

Once firmly established by the late 1970s and early 1980s on both sides of the Atlantic, it is fascinating to observe how women's soccer in the United States and football in Europe quickly became absorbed by the extant sports structures and cultures dominant on each of the two continents. On the European side, women's football quickly became the purview of clubs which – just like in the men's game – developed into the mainstay of the game's quotidian life. This existence ranged from regular matches and leagues, to championships and tournaments, from player development, coaching and training methods, to feeding each country's national team with the best players in the land. Above all, the women's game attained a clear-cut pyramidal league structure that the men's has had for well over one century with the top representing the best teams but with the relegation-promotion system allowing the bottom realistic hopes to make it to the top. All of this has come to function under the monopolistic guidance and jurisdiction of each country's football federation which, in turn is part of a larger network of a Europe-wide organization called UEFA.

In the United States, not surprisingly, it has been the world of college sports that assumed precisely the analogous function to the European club system. America's equivalent of France's Olympique Lyonnais Feminin or Germany's 1. FFC Frankfurt has been the

University of North Carolina. America's international prowess in women's soccer would be unthinkable without the college game featuring its regular season championships, tournaments, player development, training methods and coaching. America's club world has a very different organizational structure than its European counterpart. Whereas here, too, the country's federation has gained in the game's organizational importance (indeed, as mentioned, the USSF actually runs the current American professional club league in women's soccer, the NWSL), American women's soccer has assimilated to an institutional topography that is common to all American team sports: the franchise model with closed leagues far away from anything resembling a European-style pyramid. One measure of the institutional arrival of women's soccer and football in both areas is their structural adaptation to the extant sports frameworks dominating each of these respective worlds.

In many ways, the sensational proliferation and amazing growth of women's soccer over the past four decades attests to a triumph of feminism as a major democratizing force. After all, the most fundamental tenet of any democracy is the inclusion of the previously excluded. As all democratic agents, women wanted to enter structures that were by and large closed to them. Women desired to enjoy the fruits of a world that was largely, if not exclusively, ruled by men. Beginning with the events of "1968" on both sides of the Atlantic and the ensuing emancipatory movements of inclusion of which the women's movement was a crucial though not the sole participant, women dared enter and challenge a macho world of sports (culturally hegemonic team sports in particular) in which women – though far from having achieved equality – have over the past four decades successfully attained a space of their own which simply can no longer be ignored. Interestingly, but also tellingly, virtually all the activists in this emancipatory quest – namely the thousands, later millions, of women players – rarely, if ever, perceived themselves as consciously or explicitly engaged in a political movement. But the system-transforming dimension of their quiet but firm activity attests precisely to its democratizing power. The women's desire and determination to play the very same game of association football as did the men: with the same rules, the same cleats, the same ball, in the same organizations, on the same grounds, with the same teamwork, intensity and toughness was in fact an onslaught on sexism and previous exclusion. Women wanted to enjoy competition as much as men had always done. Thus, it is not at all surprising that the intense rivalry between the American and the Norwegian national teams led the players to experience something of a mutual disdain and an antipathy for each other bordering on hatred. Julie Foudy's realistic – indeed painful -- account of how she and her American teammates felt after losing to the Norwegians in the championship gold medal game of the Sydney Olympics in 2000 and how the Americans suffered after being publicly mocked and taunted by the Norwegian players who frolicked around on the field after defeating the American women in the semifinals of the second women's World Cup in Sweden in 1995, reveals very little about sisterhood and women's solidarity. But it conveys very powerfully the deep emotions associated with competition, rivalry, the sweet sensation of victory and the bitter taste of defeat that all top-level athletes, regardless of gender, experience. Foudy's words could have been written by any male sports superstar experiencing the humiliation and hurt of a major loss in a major tournament to a bitter and hated rival. Foudy wrote about soccer players pure and simple, not women soccer players; about top-level athletes at a top-level competition, not about female athletes at a female competition.[161]

In a matter of four decades, women have successfully entered the male world of association football. Though they have become the game's accomplished producers and have attained a formal equality with the men, there can be no question that women's soccer still exists in a marginalized space compared to the men's game. Above all, in the realm of following, consuming, breathing, drinking, eating, analyzing, discussing, dreaming and debating the sport, women still speak a different language than men. The last few decades have lent women a voice of their own in the global language of Association football. Whether that voice will ever become the men's equal in its sheer

[161] Julie Foudy, "Lead On!" in Brandy Chastain, *Its Not About the Bra: How to Play Hard, Play Fair, and Put the Fun Back into Competitive Sports* (New York: HarperCollins, 2004), pp. 96 - 98

quantity and assume the qualitative weight accorded to the men's I cannot even begin to guess at this time. Yet, the internationalization of the game and the diversity of its female players present another new case of emerging cosmopolitan inclusion: profound social change that reaches across former cultural boundaries, challenging formerly protected societal domains.

So much for the success story on the production side of women's soccer, the supply side as it were, the world of playing and players. But what about the consumption side of things, the following of the sport, the fandom for it? If anything, this brief book mustered evidence that the big lacuna for the women's game's cultural acceptance and equality exists on that part of the ledger not the playing field. Recall the low attendance at women's club matches in England, Germany and, though a tad better, also the United States (with the notable exception of that soccer metropolis Portland!). When the national teams are not involved at major tournaments, the attention that women's soccer has garnered remains small. I would argue that though perhaps less formidable a task than establishing presence on the playing fields, women's presence in the world of soccer – indeed sports – fandom also furnishes an ingredient in women's solid representation and participation in the cultural construct of sport. Quite possibly we could experience similarly massive shifts in women's sports consumption – and soccer fandom -- in the course of the next 3 – 4 decades as we did in the playing area in the previous four. Just like in playing, in fandom, too, men have enjoyed a century-long head start over women. Men's proficiency in sports speak can be dated to the late 18th century when cricket and golf became the first sports that deserve the sobriquet "modern".[162] In the course of the latter half of the 19th century sports really became integral to men's identities in the United States via baseball and (college) football; in Canada via ice hockey; in Britain – in so many aspects home of modern sports – via three football codes (Association; Rugby Union; and League); and cricket; in Britain's formal imperial holdings via cricket and rugby; and in her informal colonies such as continental Europe and virtually all of Latin America (excluding the Caribbean) via Association football. The content of these languages – these sports codes -- was always different but their structure and very essence quite identical. And nothing rendered them more so than their complete dominance by men: all players, owners, coaches, managers (on the production side) and followers in the form of fans, and reporters and interpreters in the form of journalists (on the consumption side) were men: A perfect case of what Paul Hoch has so powerfully called "sexual apartheid" though I would prefer the more inclusive "gender apartheid".[163]

---

[162] Here, too, I am greatly indebted to Temple University Press for so generously permitting me to use extensive parts of three pages from my book *Sportista: Female Fandom in the United States* co-authored with Emily Albertson and published by Temple University Press in 2012. The text used here hails from pages 241 to 242 in *Sportista*.

[163] Paul Hoch, *Rip Off the Big Game: The Exploitation of Sports by the Power Elite* (Garden City, NY: Anchor Books, 1972), pp. 147 - 166.

Why have sports remained our last legitimate bastion of "separate but equal?" And this starts at a very young age. When the well-known sports sociologist Michael Messner asked his AYSO soccer league in Southern California why the coed teams that had existed until 1995 in which his elder son had played when he was five years old was abolished and replaced by gender segregated teams, he was told that "'during half-times and practices, the boys and girls tend to separate into separate groups. So the league thought it would be better for team unity if we split the boys and girls into separate leagues.'"[164] The fact that Messner's suggestion – of the separate clustering of Latino and white kids during half time never leading anyone at AYSO to create ethnically segregated leagues -- was met with incredulity underlines gender's unique position as a segregating force in the world of sports, and sports alone. Our society and culture continue to tolerate a gender segregation in sports that has become unthinkable with any other collective, be it class or ethnicity or region or religion.

Title IX has been nothing short of revolutionary in permitting women access to the production of sports. But these are still performed according to a strict gender separation. Title IX has accorded women the most basic level of equality: that of quantity, but nowhere close to the much more important metric of quality. It certainly has not provided them with any kind of cultural and social equality in terms of the sports

---

[164] Michael A. Messner, "Barbie Girls versus Sea Monsters: Children Constructing Gender" in David Karen and Robert E. Washington (eds.) *The Sport and Society Reader* (New York: Routledge, 2010), p. 187.

that they produce. Why have few, if any, feminists in the United States – at least to my knowledge – never demanded that the quarterback position of the Green Bay Packers, the point guard of the Los Angeles Lakers, and the shortstop of the New York Yankees be occupied by a woman the way they have successfully lobbied that university presidents, doctors, lawyers, mathematicians, physicists, computer engineers, senators, Supreme Court justices, be women? (And it certainly is quite realistic to expect that a woman will become president of the United States before too long. One would have already attained that position were it not for the arcana of the American political system.) Or why have there not been any major movements afoot to create mixed-gendered teams beyond those in tennis's mixed double (tellingly far and away the least prestigious of the five tennis competitions and only becoming an Olympic event in 2012) and two yachting categories which – with the equestrian disciplines – furnish the only mixed-gendered teams in the summer Olympics, the global showcase of 35 different sports and almost 400 different events? In terms of team sport, there exists the Dutch game of "Korfball" a kind of basketball with two free-standing baskets with no backboards which players can circle like goals in ice hockey. This game -- quite popular in the Low Countries of Holland and Belgium where the game has the qualities of being a respectable though not central part of these countries' respective hegemonic sports cultures and extant in 67 countries worldwide under the aegis of the International Korfball Federation (IKF) -- is played by two opposing teams of four men and four women to each team in which, however, only men guard men and women guard women with passing and shooting being the only gender-integrated parts of the game thus in essence perpetuating the gender apartheid within the game itself.[165]

Why do we as a society permit such a clear gender separation – which, regardless of its sugar coating, in essence amounts to a clear second-class role for women no matter how equal their participatory numbers may be – at the highest echelons of sports, i.e. in the world of the physical that we would never tolerate in the world of the mental or intellectual or political? The equivalent in education would be for us to foster gender-integrated elementary and secondary schools, but then only allow men to enter and compete in the top four-year colleges and leading research universities with women relegated to less prestigious institutions and community colleges even though the value of their effort in terms of degrees or championships attained would be nominally equal; or, to offer an analogy from the world of politics, women would only be allowed to run for local and state though not for national offices. I wholeheartedly agree with Eileen McDonagh and Laura Pappano's emphatic argument that separate is not equal in anything, including sports.[166]

---

[165] The rules of Korfball state that "a player is allowed to switch among opponents whom he/she is defending, *as long as they are of the same sex.*" (My emphasis).

Does the logic of *citius, altius, fortius* - swifter, higher, stronger - exact our currently practiced gender apartheid that is perceived as totally legitimate at the very top level of sports since the most accomplished men will – on average and as a rule -- always run faster, jump higher, and be stronger than the most accomplished women? If we continue to define "the best", which is such an integral part of any sport, by our current criteria, then this separate but equal world will quite possibly never change. But if we construct alternate logics to what constitutes "the best" - include metrics of cooperation and style, for example, in computing winners and losers, or create truly gender-integrated teams in which the women's output would be weighted more heavily thereby creating real incentives to have the women be welcomed as positive additions to these teams, as has long been the case in intramural contests on American college campuses - then we might actually arrive at a truly integrated sports world which would thus be congruent with virtually all important public institutions of our contemporary democratic world. And then we just might reach a situation in which women's excellence on the production side of "sports" – not "women's sports" that, like use of the phrase "lady doctor" defines the normative and base-line case of sports as *not* female[167] – will by necessity create a commensurate change in women's consumption of sports thus making the female sports fan – the sportista - the norm among women and men, and not the exception.

---

[166] Eileen McDonagh and Laura Pappano, *Playing with the Boys: Why Separate is not Equal in Sports*
[167] I derive this analogy from Lori Kendall, "Nerd nation: Images of nerds in US popular culture" *International Journal of Cultural Studies*, Volume 2, Issue 2 (1999), p. 262.

Women's soccer in the United States and women's football in Europe became integral agents over the past four decades in the emancipation of women's sports – and thus women as participants and full-fledged citizens in the larger publics of liberal democracies. But emancipation is not tantamount to equality. It is the attainment of the latter that is on the agenda for the next four decades. Women's soccer in the United States and women's football in Europe will undoubtedly assume a central role and become a major agent in that worthy process as well.

149

Made in the USA
Middletown, DE
16 February 2019